ROYAL COURT

Royal Court Theatre and Talawa Theatre Company present

BLEST BE THE TIE

by **Doña Daley**

First performance at the Royal Court Jerwood Theatre Upstairs
Sloane Square, London on 15 April 2004.

BLEST BE THE TIE
by **Doña Daley**

Cast in order of appearance
Martha **Ellen Thomas**
Eunice **Marion Bailey**
Florence **Lorna Gayle**

Director **Paulette Randall**
Designer **Libby Watson**
Lighting Designer **James Farncombe**
Sound Designer **Ian Dickinson**
Music **Delroy Murray**
Assistant Director **Pat Cumper**
Casting **Lisa Makin, Amy Ball**
Production Manager **Sue Bird**
Stage Management **Rebecca Austin, Robyn Dummer**
Stage Management Work Placements **Mayowa Badejo, Laura Edwards**
Food Preparation **Pat Cumper**
Costume Supervisor **Jackie Orton**
Dialect Coach **Claudette Williams**
Company Voice Work **Patsy Rodenburg**

The Royal Court would like to thank the following for their help with this production:
Linda Bassett, Claire Benedict, Dominic Cooke, Wendy Daley and her family, Bob Hall of Anytronics Ltd,
Cecilia Noble, Martina Laird, Valerie Lilley, Dawn Walton.

THE COMPANY

Doña Daley (writer)
Theatre includes: Rock a Bye Camden (Embassy Studio); Stick Stack Stock (BAC); Weathering the Storm (West Yorkshire Playhouse); Just One Kiss (Hampstead Theatre Plays in Schools Project); The Barber Shop.
Radio includes: Weathering the Storm.
Doña attended the Royal Court International Residency in 1999. She enjoyed working with school projects and workshops as this served as a fusion of her educational background with literature and the arts.

Marion Bailey
For the Royal Court: This Is a Chair, Hush, Beside Herself, Falkland Sound, Panic.
Other theatre includes: Holes in the Skin (Chichester Festival); Normal, All of You Mine (Bush Theatre); Dance of Death (Tricycle); Cloud Nine (Old Vic); Bad Blood (The Gate); Black Snow, Man, Beast & Virtue (RNT); Red Magic (Old Red Lion); Goose Pimples (Hampstead/Garrick); Where There Is Darkness, Favourite Nights (Lyric, Hammersmith); Raspberry (Soho Poly/Edinburgh Festival); A Doll's House (Lyric, Edinburgh); The Jaws of Death, Marking Time, Guests, One of These Days (Croydon Warehouse).
Seasons at: Oldham, Canterbury & Theatre North.
Television includes: Micawber, Shades, The Thing About Vince, Under the Sun, Dalziel & Pascoe, Shine on Harvey Moon V, Casualty, Dangerfield, The Bill, A Touch of Frost, Boon, The Bretts, To Have & To Hold, Flights, Reservations, Charlie, Raspberry, Woycek, Jury, Inspector Morse, No More Dying Then, Reflections of Evil, Big Deal, Stay Lucky, Poirot.
Film includes: Mike Leigh's 2003 Untitled, I'll Be There, All or Nothing, Offending Angels, Nasty Neighbours, Psychotherapy, Meantime, Sakhararov, Way Upstream, Coppers.

Pat Cumper (assistant director)
As a writer, theatre includes: Horses of the Night (Chelsea Centre); The Fibula (TIE); Oliver and Pinocchio (Blue Mountain); The Key Game (Talawa).
Television includes: Doctors.
Radio includes: Westway, The Darker Face of the Earth, One Bright Child, Caribbean Blue, Something Understood, Voices from the Womb.
Pat has also written a play, The Rapist (Macmillan) and a novel, One Bright Child (Blackamber Books).

Ian Dickinson (sound designer)
Ian is Head of Sound at the Royal Court.
For the Royal Court: Ladybird, Notes on Falling Leaves, Loyal Women, The Sugar Syndrome, Blood, Playing the Victim, Fallout, Flesh Wound, Hitchcock Blonde (& Lyric), Black Milk, Crazyblackmuthafuckin'self, Caryl Churchill Shorts, Imprint, Mother Teresa is Dead, Push Up, Workers Writes, Fucking Games, Herons, Cutting Through the Carnival.
Other theatre includes: Port (Royal Exchange, Manchester); Night of the Soul (RSC Barbican); Eyes of the Kappa (Gate); Crime and Punishment in Dalston (Arcola Theatre); Search and Destroy (New End, Hampstead); Phaedra, Three Sisters, The Shaughraun, Writer's Cramp (Royal Lyceum, Edinburgh); The Whore's Dream (RSC Fringe, Edinburgh); As You Like It, An Experienced Woman Gives Advice, Present Laughter, The Philadelphia Story, Wolks World, Poor Superman, Martin Yesterday, Fast Food, Coyote Ugly, Prizenight (Royal Exchange, Manchester).

James Farncombe (lighting designer)
Theatre includes: Forward (Birmingham Rep); The Maths Tutor (Hampstead Theatre and Birmingham Rep); West Side Story, Death of a Salesman, Peter Pan, The Witches, Plague of Innocence, Unsuitable Girls (Leicester Haymarket Theatre); Beautiful Thing (Nottingham Playhouse); Urban Afro Saxons, Funny Black Women on the Edge (Theatre Royal, Stratford East); This Lime Tree Bower (The Belgrade, Coventry); Making Waves (Stephen Joseph Theatre, Scarborough); The Hypochondriac, Dead Funny, Popcorn (Bolton Octagon); Amy's View (Salisbury Playhouse/Royal Theatre, Northampton); Krapp's Last Tape, A Different Way Home, A Visit from Miss Prothero (Lakeside Arts Theatre, Nottingham); Goldilocks (Lyric Theatre, Hammersmith); The Blue Room, The Elephant Man (Worcester Swan Theatre); Unsuitable Girls (Sheffield Crucible); East is East, Hector's House, Women on the Verge, Move Over Moriaty (New Vic Theatre, Stoke); Bloodtide, Dead Funny, Road, Rumblefish (York Theatre Royal).

Lorna Gayle
For the Royal Court: Almost Nothing.
Other theatre includes: Stepping Out
(Southwold Summer Theatre).
Television includes: Canterbury Tales, The Bill,
Baby Mother.
Graduated from Webber Douglas Academy
March 2003.

Paulette Randall (director)
Paulette is the Artistic Director of Talawa
Theatre Company.
For Talawa: Urban Afro Saxons (Stratford East).
Other theatre includes: King Hedley II
(Tricycle/Birmingham Rep); Funny Black Women
on the Edge, Shoot to Win, Various Posse Shows
(Stratford East); Two Trains Running, Up Against
the Wall (Tricycle); The Amen Corner (Bristol
Old Vic); Sanctuary (Joint Stock); For Colored
Girls Who Have Considered Suicide When the
Rainbow is Not Enuf (BAC/Albany Empire);
Moon on a Rainbow Shawl (Nottingham).
Television includes: Kerching!, Desmond's, The
Real McCoy, Porkpie, Marvin, Comin' Atcha
(two series), Blouse and Skirt.

Ellen Thomas
Theatre includes: Twelfth Night (Royal
Exchange); A Bitter Herb (Bristol Old Vic); Amen
Corner (Tricycle Theatre/Nottingham
Playhouse); Leonara's Dance (Black Theatre
Co-operative); Moon on a Rainbow Shawl
(Almeida); The American Clock, Fuente Ovejuna
(RNT); Echo in the Bone (Lyric, Hammersmith);
Twelfth Night (Birmingham Rep); The Vagina
Monologues (national tour).
Television includes: Never Never, Active
Defence, Where There's Smoke, Ultraviolet,
London Bridge, Holding On, Kavanagh QC III,
Ruth Rendell's Simisola, Beck, Cardiac Arrest
(three series), The Lenny Henry Show, French &
Saunders, Hallelujah Anyhow, Teachers (three
series).
Film includes: South West Nine, Wonderland,
Some Voices, Secret Laughter of Women.

Libby Watson (designer)
Theatre includes: Man of Mode (Northcott
Theatre Exeter); Secret Garden, Beautiful Thing,
The Changeling, Tenant of Wildfell Hall, Arabian
Nights, Side by Side by Sondheim (Salisbury
Playhouse); Othello, Sisterly Feelings, Morning
After the Miracle, The Play Called Corpus
Christi (Guildhall); Voyagers, The Three Servants
(Croydon Warehouse); Airport 2000 (Leicester
Haymarket/Greenwich Theatre/Riverside
Studios); The Birds (Birmingham Rep); Under
Their Influence, I Dreamt I Dwelt in Marble
Halls (Tricycle Theatre); The Front Room (Oval
House); Vengeance (Hackney Empire Bullion
Rooms); The Wills's Girls (The Tobacco Factory,
Bristol); Witch, Lone Flyer, Children of the Light,
Gigolo, Call to the Sky, Accelerate, Mr & Mrs
Schultz, The Fourth Fold (Watermill Theatre);
Ready or Not, Night of the Dons, An Audience
with Angie Le Mar, Cinderella, Funny Black
Women on the Edge, Sus, Jamaica House & The
Oddest Couple, The Key Game (Stratford East);
Urban Afro Saxons (Riverside Studios).
Opera includes: Beatrice and Benedict, Comedy
on the Bridge (GSMD).

TALAWA THEATRE COMPANY

About the Company
Talawa Theatre Company is one of the UK's best-known and most prominent Black theatre companies. Founded in 1985, Talawa is a middle-scale touring theatre company. From its first production *The Black Jacobins* by Caribbean writer CLR James in 1986 to the highly topical and successful staging of *Urban Afro Saxons* in 2003, Talawa has continually sought to provide high quality productions that reflect the significant creative role of Black theatre in Britain today.

Future Developments
For the last four years, Talawa has been pursuing a Capital Project to create a new home for Black theatre on the site of the former Westminster Theatre in Victoria. The new venue will be a well-equipped, easily accessible development with a 250 seat auditorium, rehearsal, education and archive facilities.

This will be the first Black-owned and Black-managed building based producing company in the UK and will present both the company's work and the best work by other Black companies and artists. It will be a national and international focus for the training and development of Black writers, performers, creative artists and other theatre workers, raising the profile and awareness of the work of Black artists and companies and developing a new Black audience for the theatre.

Staff
Artistic Director **Paulette Randall**
General Manager **Kate Sarley**
Education Associate **Raidene Carter**
Marketing & Press **Alison Copeland**
Literary Associate **Christopher Rodriguez**
Finance **Zewditu Bekele**
Administrator **Philippa Davis**
Capital Project
Administrator **Clara Maguire**

Board Members
The Baroness Howells of St Davids (Chair)
Claudia Webbe
Dr Marie Stewart
Louis Fleming
Jenni Francis
Jack Haslam
Pax Allottey
June Baden-Semper
Margo Boye-Anawomah
Mary Lauder
Alastair Niven
Ben Thomas
Don Warrington

Education

In addition to producing award-winning plays, Talawa has a dedicated education, development and outreach programme. Attached to every Talawa production is a package of educational work ranging from resource booklets and post-show discussions to schools' residencies and workshops. There is also an annual young people's theatre programme and a number of script development services aimed at nurturing a new generation of black artists.

Forthcoming Productions

This summer, Talawa Theatre Company and The New Wolsey Theatre, Ipswich in association with the Tricycle turn their attention to *Blues For Mr. Charlie* a revival of James Baldwin's award-winning play about racism and racial violence in 1950s' America. Directed by Paulette Randall *Blues For Mr. Charlie* is a blistering display of injustice, prejudice and human nature in all its forms.

talawa

BLUES FOR MR. CHARLIE

written by James Baldwin
directed by
Paulette Randall

26 May – 5 June
New Wolsey Theatre
Ipswich

16 June – 10 July
The Tricycle Theatre

A New Wolsey Theatre, Ipswich and Talawa co-production in association with The Tricycle

www.talawa.com
www.wolseytheatre.co.uk
www.tricycle.co.uk

TYPT:04

directed and designed by
Mem Morrison

28 – 29 August

Talawa in association with The Drill Hall

www.drillhall.co.uk

THE ENGLISH STAGE COMPANY AT THE ROYAL COURT

The English Stage Company at the Royal Court opened in 1956 as a subsidised theatre producing new British plays, international plays and some classical revivals.

The first artistic director George Devine aimed to create a writers' theatre, 'a place where the dramatist is acknowledged as the fundamental creative force in the theatre and where the play is more important than the actors, the director, the designer'. The urgent need was to find a contemporary style in which the play, the acting, direction and design are all combined. He believed that 'the battle will be a long one to continue to create the right conditions for writers to work in'.

Devine aimed to discover 'hard-hitting, uncompromising writers whose plays are stimulating, provocative and exciting'. The Royal Court production of John Osborne's Look Back in Anger in May 1956 is now seen as the decisive starting point of modern British drama and the policy created a new generation of British playwrights. The first wave included John Osborne, Arnold Wesker, John Arden, Ann Jellicoe, N F Simpson and Edward Bond. Early seasons included new international plays by Bertolt Brecht, Eugène Ionesco, Samuel Beckett, Jean-Paul Sartre and Marguerite Duras.

The theatre started with the 400-seat proscenium arch Theatre Downstairs, and then in 1969 opened a second theatre, the 60-seat studio Theatre Upstairs. Some productions transfer to the West End, such as Terry Johnson's Hitchcock Blonde, Caryl Churchill's Far Away, Conor McPherson's The Weir, Kevin Elyot's Mouth to Mouth and My Night With Reg. The Royal Court also co-produces plays which have transferred to the West End or toured internationally, such as Sebastian Barry's The Steward of Christendom and Mark Ravenhill's Shopping and Fucking (with Out of Joint), Martin McDonagh's The Beauty Queen Of Leenane (with Druid Theatre Company), Ayub Khan Din's East is East (with Tamasha Theatre Company, and now a feature film).

Since 1994 the Royal Court's artistic policy has again been vigorously directed to finding and producing a new generation of playwrights. The writers include Joe Penhall, Rebecca Prichard, Michael Wynne, Nick Grosso, Judy Upton, Meredith Oakes, Sarah Kane, Anthony Neilson, Judith Johnson, James Stock, Jez Butterworth, Marina Carr, Phyllis Nagy, Simon Block, Martin McDonagh, Mark Ravenhill, Ayub Khan Din, Tamantha Hammerschlag, Jess Walters, Ché Walker, Conor McPherson,

photo: Andy Chopping

Simon Stephens, Richard Bean, Roy Williams, Gary Mitchell, Mick Mahoney, Rebecca Gilman, Christopher Shinn, Kia Corthron, David Gieselmann, Marius von Mayenburg, David Eldridge, Leo Butler, Zinnie Harris, Grae Cleugh, Roland Schimmelpfennig, DeObia Oparei, Vassily Sigarev, the Presnyakov Brothers and Lucy Prebble. This expanded programme of new plays has been made possible through the support of A.S.K Theater Projects and the Skirball Foundation, the Jerwood Charitable Foundation, the American Friends of the Royal Court Theatre and many in association with the Royal National Theatre Studio.

In recent years there have been record-breaking productions at the box office, with capacity houses for Roy Williams' Fallout, Terry Johnson's Hitchcock Blonde, Caryl Churchill's A Number, Jez Butterworth's The Night Heron, Rebecca Gilman's Boy Gets Girl, Kevin Elyot's Mouth to Mouth, David Hare's My Zinc Bed and Conor McPherson's The Weir, which transferred to the West End in October 1998 and ran for nearly two years at the Duke of York's Theatre.

The newly refurbished theatre in Sloane Square opened in February 2000, with a policy still inspired by the first artistic director George Devine. The Royal Court is an international theatre for new plays and new playwrights, and the work shapes contemporary drama in Britain and overseas.

AWARDS FOR THE ROYAL COURT

Jez Butterworth won the 1995 George Devine Award, the Writers' Guild New Writer of the Year Award, the Evening Standard Award for Most Promising Playwright and the Olivier Award for Best Comedy for Mojo.

The Royal Court was the overall winner of the 1995 Prudential Award for the Arts for creativity, excellence, innovation and accessibility. The Royal Court Theatre Upstairs won the 1995 Peter Brook Empty Space Award for innovation and excellence in theatre.

Michael Wynne won the 1996 Meyer-Whitworth Award for The Knocky. Martin McDonagh won the 1996 George Devine Award, the 1996 Writers' Guild Best Fringe Play Award, the 1996 Critics' Circle Award and the 1996 Evening Standard Award for Most Promising Playwright for The Beauty Queen of Leenane. Marina Carr won the 19th Susan Smith Blackburn Prize (1996/7) for Portia Coughlan. Conor McPherson won the 1997 George Devine Award, the 1997 Critics' Circle Award and the 1997 Evening Standard Award for Most Promising Playwright for The Weir. Ayub Khan-Din won the 1997 Writers' Guild Awards for Best West End Play and Writers' Guild New Writer of the Year and the 1996 John Whiting Award for East is East (co-production with Tamasha).

At the 1998 Tony Awards, Martin McDonagh's The Beauty Queen of Leenane (co-production with Druid Theatre Company) won four awards including Garry Hynes for Best Director and was nominated for a further two. Eugene Ionesco's The Chairs (co-production with Theatre de Complicite) was nominated for six Tony awards. David Hare won the 1998 Time Out Live Award for Outstanding Achievement and six awards in New York including the Drama League, Drama Desk and New York Critics Circle Award for Via Dolorosa. Sarah Kane won the 1998 Arts Foundation Fellowship in Playwriting. Rebecca Prichard won the 1998 Critics' Circle Award for Most Promising Playwright for Yard Gal (co-production with Clean Break).

Conor McPherson won the 1999 Olivier Award for Best New Play for The Weir. The Royal Court won the 1999 ITI Award for Excellence in International Theatre. Sarah Kane's Cleansed was judged Best Foreign Language Play in 1999 by Theater Heute in Germany. Gary Mitchell won the 1999 Pearson Best Play Award for Trust. Rebecca Gilman was joint winner of the 1999 George Devine Award and won the 1999 Evening Standard Award for Most Promising Playwright for The Glory of Living.

In 1999, the Royal Court won the European theatre prize New Theatrical Realities, presented at Taormina Arte in Sicily, for its efforts in recent years in discovering and producing the work of young British dramatists.

Roy Williams and Gary Mitchell were joint winners of the George Devine Award 2000 for Most Promising Playwright for Lift Off and The Force of Change respectively. At the Barclays Theatre Awards 2000 presented by the TMA, Richard Wilson won the Best Director Award for David Gieselmann's Mr Kolpert and Jeremy Herbert won the Best Designer Award for Sarah Kane's 4.48 Psychosis. Gary Mitchell won the Evening Standard's Charles Wintour Award 2000 for Most Promising Playwright for The Force of Change. Stephen Jeffreys' I Just Stopped by to See the Man won an AT&T: On Stage Award 2000.

David Eldridge's Under the Blue Sky won the Time Out Live Award 2001 for Best New Play in the West End. Leo Butler won the George Devine Award 2001 for Most Promising Playwright for Redundant. Roy Williams won the Evening Standard's Charles Wintour Award 2001 for Most Promising Playwright for Clubland. Grae Cleugh won the 2001 Olivier Award for Most Promising Playwright for Fucking Games. Richard Bean was joint winner of the George Devine Award 2002 for Most Promising Playwright for Under the Whaleback. Caryl Churchill won the 2002 Evening Standard Award for Best New Play for A Number. Vassily Sigarev won the 2002 Evening Standard Charles Wintour Award for Most Promising Playwright for Plasticine. Ian MacNeil won the 2002 Evening Standard Award for Best Design for A Number and Plasticine. Peter Gill won the 2002 Critics' Circle Award for Best New Play for The Yoke Realist (English Touring Theatre). Ché Walker won the 2003 George Devine Award for Most Promising Playwright for Flesh Wound. Lucy Prebble won the 2003 Critics' Circle Award for Most Promising Playwright.

ROYAL COURT BOOKSHOP

The Royal Court bookshop offers a diverse selection of contemporary plays and publications on the theory and practice of modern drama. The staff specialise in assisting with the selection of audition monologues and scenes.
Royal Court playtexts from past and present productions cost £2.
The Bookshop is situated in the downstairs ROYAL COURT BAR AND FOOD.
Monday–Friday 3–10pm, Saturday 2–10pm
For information tel: 020 7565 5024
or email: bookshop@royalcourttheatre.com

THE AMERICAN FRIENDS OF THE ROYAL COURT THEATRE

AFRCT support the mission of the Royal Court and are primarily focused on raising funds to enable the theatre to produce new work by emerging American writers. Since this not-for-profit organisation was founded in 1997, AFRCT have contributed to ten productions. They have also supported the participation of young artists in the Royal Court's acclaimed International Residency.

If you would like to support the ongoing work of the Royal Court, please contact the Development Department on 020 7565 5050.

AMERICAN FRIENDS
Founders
Francis Finlay
Amanda Foreman and Jonathan Barton
Monica Gerard-Sharp & Ali Wambold
Mary Ellen Johnson & Richard Goeltz
Dany Khosrovani
Blythe Masters
Laura Pels
Ben Rauch and Margaret Scott
Mr & Mrs Gerald Schoenfeld

Patrons
Catherine Curran
William & Ursula Fairbairn
Francis H. Goldwyn
Mr & Mrs Richard Grand
Sahra Lese
Imelda Liddiard

Benefactors
Rachael Bail
Jeff & Cynthia Penney
Tim Runion & Vipul Nishawala
Mike Sterling

Members
Harry Brown & Richard Walsh
Georgiana Ellis
Christopher Flacke
Nancy Flinn
Jennifer R. Gardner
Sharon King Hoge
Nancy Lamb
Rochelle Ohrstrom
Evelyn Renold
Roberta Schneiderman
David and Patricia Smalley

Corporations and Foundations
American Express Company
Bates Worldwide
The Blessing Way Foundation
The Howard Gilman Foundation
The Magowan Family Foundation
The Laura Pels Foundation
The Sy Syms Foundation
Union Pacific Corporation

American Friends
Development Director
Timothy Runion
Tel: +1 212 946 5724

ROYAL COURT
SLOANE SQUARE

Jerwood Theatre Downstairs

4 June – 17 July
SHINING CITY
written and directed by **Conor McPherson**
A Royal Court and Gate Theatre Dublin production

Jerwood Theatre Upstairs

14 May – 12 June
LUCKY DOG
by **Leo Butler**
directed by **James Macdonald**
cast includes: **Linda Bassett**

24 June – 17 July
COUNTRY MUSIC
by **Simon Stephens**
directed by **Gordon Anderson**

A Royal Court and ATC co-production

BOX OFFICE
020 7565 5000

PROGRAMME SUPPORTERS

The Royal Court (English Stage Company Ltd) receives its principal funding from Arts Council England, London. It is also supported financially by a wide range of private companies and public bodies and earns the remainder of its income from the box office and its own trading activities. The Royal Borough of Kensington & Chelsea gives an annual grant to the Royal Court Young Writers' Programme.
The Genesis Foundation supports the International Season and Young Writers Festival.

The Jerwood Charitable Foundation supports new plays by new playwrights through the Jerwood New Playwrights series. The Skirball Foundation fund a Playwrights' Programme at the theatre. The Artistic Director's Chair is supported by a lead grant from The Peter Jay Sharp Foundation, contributing to the activities of the Artistic Director's office. Bloomberg Mondays, the Royal Court's reduced price ticket scheme, is supported by Bloomberg. Over the past seven years the BBC has supported the Gerald Chapman Fund for directors.

ROYAL COURT
DEVELOPMENT BOARD
Tamara Ingram (Chair)
Jonathan Cameron (Vice Chair)
Timothy Burrill
Anthony Burton
Jonathan Caplan QC
Sindy Caplan
Mark Crowdy
Joseph Fiennes
Joyce Hytner
Dan Klein
Gavin Neath
Michael Potter
Ben Rauch
Kadee Robbins
Mark Robinson
William Russell
Sue Stapely
James L Tanner
Will Turner

TRUSTS AND FOUNDATIONS
American Friends of the Royal Court Theatre
Gerald Chapman Fund
Cowley Charitable Trust
The Dorset Foundation
The Foundation for Sport and the Arts
The Foyle Foundation
Francis Finlay Foundation
Genesis Foundation
The Haberdashers' Company
Jerwood Charitable Foundation
The Boris Karloff Charitable Foundation
John Lyon's Charity
The Magowan Family Foundation
The Moose Foundation for the Arts
The Diana Parker Charitable Trust
The Laura Pels Foundation
Quercus Charitable Trust
The Peter Jay Sharp Foundation
Skirball Foundation

SPONSORS
American Airlines
Arts & Business New Partners
Barclays

BBC
Bloomberg
Peter Jones
Royal College of Psychiatrists

BUSINESS MEMBERS
Aviva plc
Burberry
Lazard
Pemberton Greenish
Simons Muirhead & Burton
Slaughter and May

MEDIA MEMBERS
Beatwax
Bloomsbury
Columbia Tristar Films (UK)
Hat Trick Productions
Miramax Films
XL Video UK

PRODUCTION SYNDICATE
Anonymous
The Albano Family
Jonathan & Sindy Caplan
Kay Hartenstein Saatchi
Richard & Susan Hayden
Peter & Edna Goldstein
Jack & Linda Keenan
Kadee Robbins
The Viscount & Viscountess Rothermere
William & Hilary Russell
Jan & Michael Topham

INDIVIDUAL MEMBERS
Patrons
Anonymous
Katie Bradford
Marcus J Burton
Ms Kay Ellen Consolver
Mrs Philip Donald
Celeste Fenichel
Tom & Simone Fenton
Jack & Linda Keenan
Richard & Robin Landsberger
Duncan Matthews QC
Ian & Carol Sellars
Jan & Michael Topham
Richard Wilson OBE

Benefactors
Anonymous
Martha Allfrey
Lucy Bryn Davies

Jeremy Conway & Nicola Van Gelder
Robyn Durie
Winstone & Jean Fletcher
Joachim Fleury
Homevale Ltd.
Tamara Ingram
Peter & Maria Kellner
Barbara Minto
Nigel Seale
Jenny Sheridan
Brian D Smith
Amanda Vail
Sir Robert & Lady Wilson

Associates
Anonymous
Anastasia Alexander
Brian Boylan
Mr & Mrs M Bungey
Ossi & Paul Burger
Mrs Helena Butler
Lady Cazalet
Carole & Neville Conrad
David & Susan Coppard
Margaret Cowper
Barry Cox
Andrew Cryer
Linda & Ronald F. Daitz
David Day
Zoë Dominic
Kim Dunn
Charlotte & Nick Fraser
Jacqueline & Jonathan Gestetner
Vivien Goodwin
Judy & Frank Grace
Don & Sue Guiney
P. Hobbs - LTRC
Mrs Ellen Josefowitz
David Kaskel & Christopher Teano
Mr & Mrs Tarek Kassem
Carole A. Leng
Lady Lever
Colette & Peter Levy
Mr Watcyn Lewis
David Marks
Nicola McFarland
Rod & Mina McManigal
Eva Monley
Gavin & Ann Neath
Georgia Oetker
Mr & Mrs Michael Orr
Pauline Pinder

William Plapinger & Cassie Murray
William Poeton CBE & Barbara Poeton
Jan & Michael Potter
Jeremy Priestley
Beverley Rider
Lois Sieff OBE
Sue Stapely
Will Turner
Anthony Wigram

FOR THE ROYAL COURT

Royal Court Theatre, Sloane Square, London SW1W 8AS
Tel: 020 7565 5050 Fax: 020 7565 5001
info@royalcourttheatre.com
www.royalcourttheatre.com

Artistic Director **Ian Rickson**
Associate Director International **Elyse Dodgson**
Associate Director **Marianne Elliott**+
Associate Director Casting **Lisa Makin**
Associate Directors* **Stephen Daldry, James Macdonald, Katie Mitchell, Max Stafford-Clark, Richard Wilson**
Literary Manager **Graham Whybrow**
Pearson Playwright **Leo Butler**†
Voice Associate **Patsy Rodenburg***
Casting Assistant **Amy Ball**
International Administrator **Ushi Bagga**
International Associate **Ramin Gray**
Artistic Assistant **Polly Wines**

Production Manager **Paul Handley**
Deputy Production Manager **Sue Bird**
Production Assistant **Hannah Bentley**
Facilities Manager **Fran McElroy**
Head of Lighting **Johanna Town**
Lighting Deputy **Trevor Wallace**
Assistant Electricians **James Glanville, Gavin Owen**
Lighting Board Operator **Sam Shortt**
Head of Stage **Martin Riley**
Stage Deputy **Steven Stickler**
Stage Chargehand **Daniel Lockett**
Head of Sound **Ian Dickinson**
Sound Deputy **Emma Laxton**
Head of Wardrobe **Iona Kenrick**
Wardrobe Deputy **Jackie Orton**

YOUNG WRITERS PROGRAMME
Associate Director **Ola Animashawun**
Administrator **Nina Lyndon**
Outreach Worker **Lucy Dunkerley**
Education Officer **Emily McLaughlin**
Writers Tutor **Simon Stephens***
Trainee Associate Director **Joe Hill-Gibbins**§

General Manager **Diane Borger**
Administrator **Nia Janis**
Finance Director **Sarah Preece**
Finance Officer **Rachel Harrison***
Finance Assistant **Martin Wheeler**
Finance Accountant **Carol Daniel***

Head of Marketing **Penny Mills**
Head of Press **Ewan Thomson**
Marketing Officer **Alix Hearn**
Press Officer **Claire Gascoyne**
Box Office Manager **Neil Grutchfield**
Deputy Box Office Manager **Valli Dakshinamurthi**
Duty Box Office Manager **Glen Bowman**
Box Office Sales Operators **Susanna Greenwood, Louise Kelly, Steven Kuleshnyk**

Head of Development **Helen Salmon**
Development Manager **Rebecca Preston***
Trusts and Foundations Manager **Nicky Jones**
Sponsorship Officer **Chris James**

Theatre Manager **Elizabeth Brown**
Front of House Managers **Dermot Sellars, Bobbie Stokes**
Duty House Managers* **Alan Gilmour, Matt Tallen, David Duchin**
Bookshop Manager **Simon David**
Assistant Bookshop Manager **Edin Suljic***
Bookshop Assistants* **Elly Thomas, Nicki Welburn**
Stage Door/Reception **Simon David, Jon Hunter, Tyrone Lucas.**

Thanks to all of our box office assistants and ushers.

+ The Associate Director post is supported by the BBC through the Gerald Chapman Fund.
§ The Trainee Associate Director Bursary is supported by the Quercus Trust.
† This theatre has the support of the Pearson Playwright's Scheme sponsored by Pearson plc.
* Part-time.

ENGLISH STAGE COMPANY

President
Sir John Mortimer CBE QC

Vice President
Joan Plowright CBE

Honorary Council
Sir Richard Eyre
Alan Grieve

Council
Chairwoman **Liz Calder**
Vice Chairman **Anthony Burton**

Members
Judy Daish
Graham Devlin
Joyce Hytner
Tamara Ingram
Stephen Jeffreys
Phyllida Lloyd
James Midgley
Edward Miliband
Sophie Okonedo
Katharine Viner

Blest Be the Tie

Doña Daley

ROYAL COURT

First published in 2004 by the Royal Court Theatre
(English Stage Company Ltd), Sloane Square, London SW1W 8AS

Typeset by Country Setting, Kingsdown, Kent CT14 8ES
Printed in England by Intype London Ltd

All rights reserved

Copyright © Doña Daley, 2002

Doña Daley is herby identified as the author
of this work in accordance with Section 77
of the Copyright, Designers and Patents Act 1988

All rights whatsoever in this work are strictly reserved.
Applications for permission for any use whatsoever, including
performance rights must be made in advance, prior to any
such proposed use, c/o The Administrator, Royal Court Theatre,
Sloane Square, London SW1W 8AS. No performance may
be given unless a licence first been obtained

*This book is sold subject to the condition that it shall not,
by way of trade or otherwise, be lent, resold, hired out or
otherwise circulated without the publisher's prior consent
in any form of binding or cover other than that in which
it is published and without a similar condition including
this condition being imposed on the subsequent purchaser*

A CIP record for this book
is available from the British Library

ISBN 0-946303-11-8

2 4 6 8 10 9 7 5 3 1

Characters

Florence

Martha

Eunice

This playscript was correct at the time of going to press, but may not include all changes made during rehearsal.

Scene One

We see a woman in her mid- to late-fifties: Martha (or Cherise as she now calls herself).

She is standing in the middle of a cramped room in a council flat. She has a large suitcase with her and a trophy. She has just arrived. We hear her say 'Thanks,' and the front door is slammed shut. She looks around the room, and it is obvious from her demeanour that she is shocked at what she sees. She looks intently around the room as she sits down. Lights fade.

Scene Two

We see the same room as in Scene One. This is Florence's home: it is quite small, and there are too many things in the room, which makes it feel claustrophobic. Some of the things have been moved around slightly since the previous scene. On the wall are pictures of family and religious scenes, a picture of Jesus' bleeding heart the most prominent. There is a large old-fashioned sofa and heavy chairs. At stage right there is a door to a balcony. The large ostentatious trophy that Martha had, some three feet high, now stands in one corner of the room.

We hear a 'Trisha' programme on the television. It is about jealousy in the family and how members feel they are being treated. There is a great deal of commotion and shouting.

The lights rise and we see a white woman, Eunice, in her mid- to late-fifties (but looking older than her years). She is snoozing in a wing chair. This is not her own home, but she appears to feel at home. There is a kitchen (centre back), door open, and we see several saucepans on the stove, cooking and bubbling slowly.

The woman wakes with a start. Her first concern is to check whether her cooking has been spoiled. When satisfied that this is not the case, she checks the time, watches what is on the television for a moment, checks all the channels to see if there is anything better, and settles to finish watching what is left of the 'Trisha' programme.

Eunice That's right, give it to them straight! That's right.

We see her generally tidying around and fussing. She is obviously expecting visitors. She goes to the sideboard, takes out a tablecloth, table-mats and cutlery, and begins to set the table, She stops a moment, then returns the items to where she got them from. The phone rings.

Eunice Hello? . . . Yes? Oh it's you . . . No, Martha . . . sorry! She hasn't come back yet . . . No, I didn't say anything . . . No, I won't say anything . . . Where are you now? . . . Very nice . . . Good . . . She rang me not so long ago . . . Said she was at Victoria . . . Oh, another few minutes I should think . . . She won't be long . . . That's right . . . Alright . . . Alright . . . See you later . . . No . . . I won't say anything . . . (*Puts the phone down.*)

Somewhat restless, she checks her saucepans again, turns one or two off and returns to her chair. She examines her camera to see if the flash is working and that she has enough film in it. Just as she sits down she hears the door. Florence, a black woman in her late-sixties or early-seventies, has just returned from a few days away at her daughter's in Manchester.

Florence (*offstage by the front door*) Eunice, is you dat?

Eunice Who do you think it is? (*Switches off the television.*)

Florence Tank God! Help me out here me dear mam! Come! Come! Bring the Dettol and a rag.

Eunice does as she is told, getting the items from the kitchen. She goes to the front door and returns with a wheelie suitcase.

Florence (*enters the room in her stockinged feet*) Nasty set a people dem! What a homecoming! Haf fe stand in a piss! Dem soon shit inna de place too! A dem man from upstairs yu know.

Eunice Well you don't know . . .

Florence Yes me sure a dat. When dem come from de pub and can't wait till dem reach dem flat on de fourteenth floor dem must relieve them self by de twelfth. And lef de place like paddling pool fe me fe stand inna! Me so glad yu was here fe help me out. (*She is writing a notice.*)

Eunice What's that yer doing?

Florence Been tinking 'bout dis fe a long time!

She shows Eunice a sign that says 'Piss in This!' She goes to the balcony and returns with a very large ceramic vase. She looks at it, takes the sign from Eunice and adds: 'And empty it when you done.'

Eunice You can't do that!

Florence Something got to be done, man. De Council nah tek dis ting in hand. Me fed up of this. All the time I been living here is the same ting! Too much of one ting good fe nothing, man! If I could a get out of dis place yu see?

Eunice Got that off yer chest then! Cup of tea?

Florence Alright. Feel little better. Is what you doing here? (*She goes out to the lift with her notice and the vase.*)

Eunice There's a very good reason! How was your journey?

Florence (*returning*) Not bad! Have one Scottish woman sit next to me all the way. Or maybe Irish? I don't really know. All me know seh I don't understand one word de woman was saying. Is why dese people nu talk straight so yu can understand them? She rest herself beside me and me hear – (*Imitating something akin to a Scottish accent.*) 'Ruh! Ruh ruh,' and she laugh. So me smile too! Nuh want her believe seh me unfriendly!

Eunice 'Course not.

Florence But dat put me in a worries.

Eunice Oh?

Florence For the likkle smile me smile wid her encourage her! For she start the 'Ruh ruh' all the way from Manchester to London! Me pick out one and two word . . . me hear Glasgow (mus is dere she come from or dere she live) den she bring out picture (believe seh a the grand kids dem). Den me a realise that de 'Ruh! Ruh!' change.

Eunice Really?

Florence Yes! And when me realise de woman must did ask me question. For she a look up inna me face! But the ting was me never know seh what she ask me!

Eunice What did you do?

Florence I just smile and use me best English and seh, 'I don't really know.' She did seem satisfy wid dat. Me get more dan small talk pan me journey!

Eunice Oh?

Florence Hey! Hey de small talk turn inna a long talk! No way round it but to endure fe de whole journey! So how yu be?

She goes to place her handbag on a small table that has been moved. Florence is perplexed by this and puts the table back to its original place.

Eunice I'm alright . . .

Florence So what yu doing here today? We never plan fe meet.

Eunice Well, I thought I'd come over and welcome you back . . . and . . .

Florence Me glad fe see yu all de same . . . A whey dis? (*Seeing the trophy in the corner. At the same time a clock strikes four.*) And dis? Eunice, yu must stop give me tings! Me don't know if me can live wid dis thing a mek noise all de while!

Eunice Well . . .

Florence Me nu have room fe nuttin else inna dis likkle place! Is what? (*Indicates the trophy.*) Light stand? Light stand or something?

Eunice No. I didn't bring it.

Florence Then is who? Don't tell me seh Angela tink me woulda like dis!

Eunice Well, I'm not supposed to say anything . . .

Florence What yu talking about?

Eunice It's a surprise all of this . . . you see . . .

Florence A surprise fe true! Den why it never hide? Not my kind a ting at all. Don't even suit inna de place. Too big! Too big and brash! . . .

Eunice (*interrupting*) STOP NU! Can't have room fe talk! You've got a visitor!

Florence Like who? Nobody come here again. Me is the one that do the visiting. Is who? Is who a visit?

Eunice Some one from a long way away.

Florence A whey dis? A game show we deh pan? Talk! Talk Nu! Is who?

Eunice Someone called Cherise has come to see you.

Florence Cherise? Cherise? Me don't know nu Cherise!

Eunice Oh you do . . .

Florence Seh what?

Eunice Passing through London, apparently. Thought she would look you up . . . That's nice.

Florence Yu tink so. Is what she want? Whey she come from? Why she come? How she know me?

Eunice Came three days ago. You just missed her. Was here for some hairdressing competition or something. That's one of her prizes . . . I'll expect she'll tell yer all about it when she gets in.

Florence Is how she find me?

Eunice Got yer address. Got here in a taxi to find you weren't in. Them next door told her about me and I let her in!

Florence What she woulda do if yu wasn't dere?

Eunice I did the right thing, didn't I? Not like it was a stranger or anything – showed me a picture of you on holiday in Jamaica. You, her and your mother. Lovely picture of you. Never seen that one meself.

Florence Me she and me mother? (*Pondering.*) Me never tek any picture except wid me sister and me, nu hear from de wutliss gal fe de longest while. Mark you, she wouldn't have money fe come. So what dis person seh she want?

Eunice Think about it. You know this person.

Florence Me sister? She name Martha. A Martha she call. Yu feget?

Eunice Changed her name by all accounts. Likes to be called Cherise now.

Florence Seh what? What she want?

Eunice Strange question. (*Beat.*) To see you of course!

Florence Me nuh hear from her fe de longest while, How she reach? Whey she get money? A wonder if she involve inna drugs sinting? Me hear how Jamaican woman turn themselves into donkey and a carry drugs.

Eunice Mules! That's what they call them. I don't think there is anything like that going on.

Florence All the letter that me write never get no reply. Parcel send every year. As me a talk. A little something for you!

She takes some towels and toiletries out of her case. She gives a a little bundle of things to Eunice and puts the rest in a box behind the sofa.

Eunice Oh ta! What a lovely colour!

Florence Marks and Spencer cast-off, de man tell me! Still have the label but less dan half de price. Feel how dem soft! A market me get dem! Have some fe de parcel! Martha will like them, me sure of that.

Eunice You will be able to give them to her in person this year! I've never been sure why you bothered keep sending the parcel. And now that I've seen her . . .

Florence I would feel bad. Dem need the things and it save dem pocket.

Eunice Yeah, and drains yours, you're a pensioner now, you can't be expected to keep this up for ever!

Florence It's expected me dear mam, it's expected. Tek the young lady Martha now, first time I used to hear from her nuff time. 'Sis, I'm begging yu to send shampoo or setters or Avalon Hair Cream.' No money! Me must send dese tings.

Eunice Yes! Quite. Just like in ours. At least Eddie is still working.

Florence Me one sister and she don't correspond? After me write how much letter wid news and enquiring how she and the children be and me don't get no reply, me stop write so often yah sah! Me don't know no one a Jamaica again!

Eunice Except at Christmas.

Florence 'To my Loving Sister at Christmas!' That's de thanks me get fe me Christmas box whey me send. Fe over forty years every year de big parcel. Mek sure dem have a good Christmas. Since Mama dead is just the card and nothing else. Dat a news? How she know seh me still 'loving'?

Eunice But you are! Aren't you?

Florence (*grunts*) Me nuh have money fe entertain visitors.

Eunice I don't think you'll have any problem there. She looked very well-to-do to me.

Florence Don't mek what yu see pan de outside fool yu. She coming from Jamaica, Eunice . . . people like Martha don't have money. Last time I see her she had a likkle piece of place at Crossroads in Kingston a do people hair. Few dollars a head and living in two rooms behind the shop wid her children. Me know she move . . . but I don't know de place . . .

Eunice Nice that she's come though . . . isn't it?

Florence I don't know if I glad or sorry. See how she stay! Spring herself pan me . . . no word or anything! Don't know me situation. Look pan de place. Woulda better if she stay wid Angela. She could use the en-suite at Angela's. She would be more comfortable.

Eunice You can't pack her off to Docklands! What would she do there all day?

Florence I business?

Eunice Then it's the trek to see her.

Florence Angela could bring her when she finish work.

Eunice You know you can't do that. She's family, she'll have to muck in . . .

Florence How long she say she staying?

Eunice She didn't say exactly . . .

Florence Since she seh she passing through, maybe just for a week or so. I tink I can manage dat. Me nu so sure I in the mood for visitors right now.

Eunice Well, she's here now . . .

Florence Come and set down herself on me after what? Fifteen years?

Martha has let herself in at this point and is standing at the door. She has an assortment of bags. She has been shopping.

Martha Fe yu memory bad eh? A nearly thirty years since fe we eye mek four! Sis? (*Beat.*) How yu do?

Florence Martha! You reach? You look nice. Yu look very nice!

Martha Try me a try me darlin'.

The two women hug. Martha nods in Eunice's direction.

Eunice. So yu let out de secret?

Eunice Your trophy gave it away!

Martha Should a keep quiet all de same.

Florence Me and Eunice don't keep secret.

Eunice Come on, take your coat off. Dinner is virtually ready!

Florence Everything ready?

Martha I woulda cook, but Eunice did insist.

Eunice Can't have visitors cooking! The day I can't put a little food on a table that's the day that they take me out feet first! (*Lets out a little laugh.*)

Florence Stop yu noise!

Eunice It's the truth. Can't beat a good meal inside yer after a journey.

Martha You have a nice time in Manchester? How are the grandkids?

Florence Thriving. Bella is so bright. De baby doing very well. Fay so happy and settled. Justin treat her good.

Eunice That's nice.

Florence Yes man.

Eunice Me all get picture fe me wall. Good drawing fe eight, yu don't tink so? (*Produces the picture.*) Fay have a lovely house. Big garden for Bella to play in. She is doing well. Very well. Gwine give her a next important job pan de paper. She seem very happy 'bout it. Have live-in nanny now.

Eunice Oh I say.

Florence Yes me dear! Fay seh I mus' leave London and come live wid her!

Eunice Did she now?

Martha That's good to hear. Someone to look after you.

Eunice But what would you do in Manchester? It's so cold up there . . .

Florence Me nah move yah sah! Me can look after meself.

Eunice That's good!

Florence Yes. Yes. So yu mek yuself comfortable.

Martha I beg Miss Eunice to help me out while you was away.

Eunice A few directions. That's all. I sorted out the spare room. Dumped everything into your room, I'm afraid!

Florence Well, bein' as I wasn't expecting visitors, tings not all that straight. Yu never give me notice. Is how yu reach?

Martha Well, I'm here on a official business! Came over for the World Black Hairstyle Competition and Convention! At a place called Something Palace.

Eunice Alexandra.

Martha Dat's it. See me prize? First prize for the most original style and colouring technique. Come clear from Jamaica and win prize a England!

Florence Imagine. (*Looking at the trophy more closely.*) Number One. Number One in the World!

Martha So dem seh! My dear.

Florence (*reading the inscription*) Cherise Sylvester. So what wrong wid de name yu born and grow wid?

Martha Sounds better. Has a certain style and class.

Florence Martha Williams sound alright to me.

Martha Dat was de advise me get. I follow and see it dere!

Florence I see. (*Beat.*) What leave to do, Eunice?

Eunice Nothing, I'm telling you. Mind you, table will need setting.

Florence Bless you!

Martha You want me do anything, Sis? Eunice do so much areddy she must want to get home.

Florence No. Rest you'self.

Eunice I'll do it. Might as well finish the job. Then I'll go. (*Has to push past Martha to get to the sideboard.*)

Martha I in your way!

Eunice Don't you worry yourself. Can't swing a cat in these places. Mind you, not allowed to keep one, let alone swing one.

Martha Seh what?

Eunice Built them to house as many as they could. Weren't thinking that space would be needed for all our stuff. Were they, Florence?

Florence (*from the kitchen*) What that yu saying?

Eunice I was telling Martha that the Council just wanted to make sure that we had somewhere to stop, not thinking that we would need a little space as well.

Florence That is the truth. Remember how the front room in Ingrave Street used to swallow up the three-piece?

Eunice Now the three-piece swallows up the room!

They both laugh.

Florence Can't get rid of it!

Eunice I know . . . You know something M – (*Corrects herself.*) Cherise. She had just made the last payment on this when we got the notice that they were going to pull our houses down.

Florence Just got the front room nice . . . and then . . .

Eunice Way it goes . . .

Martha Could have get another one. Something smaller.

Eunice Not that easy then, was it, Florence? All that early morning cleaning at Arding and Hobbs . . . Still . . .

Florence So I hang on to the settee. (*Beat.*) You going to stay?

Eunice I wasn't planning to. I only cooked enough for two. I must get back. Eddie is on mornings. I like to be there when he gets home.

Florence Not even for a cup of tea? Stay, man, I mek the tea areddy! Coffee fe yu, Martha? I remember seh yu don't tek tea.

Martha No tanks.

Eunice I'll stop for a drink with yer. Set me on me way.

Martha Yu don't have far to go!

Eunice You're not wrong. (*To Martha.*) Can wave to her from my balcony.

Florence comes out with two cups of tea.

Florence! There's not enough sugar in this. Give us that spoon!

Florence But yu feget what they say at the clinic, you must cut down.

Eunice Forget it! I've always had three sugars and that's the way its going to be. I've a long way to go before I'm sweet enough.

Florence Sweet for what?

Eunice Eddie's not done with me yet! (*Laughs heartily. Notices that Martha is surprised by her comment.*) Well, Martha, no doubt I'll be seeing a lot more of you. Six months is a long holiday!

Florence How long? (*Nearly drops her cup.*)

Martha Well, that's how long the ticket open for. We'll see what happen. Didn't want to make no plan. Thought it would be nice to spend time with you. Don't see yu fe de longest while. A little surprise

Florence Me get that all right. Yu can leave tings at home for so long?

Martha I have people who can take care of tings fe me. Me hardly spend time in the shop dem now, you know.

Florence Shop dem. You still have the likkle place a Crossroads? Right?

Martha Close dat long time, man. Gawn uptown now. Where the real money is.

Florence Eh! And have uptown name fe go wid it!

Martha So it go, my dear.

Eunice You've lots to catch up on, I suppose. Well, you haven't come for the weather, have you?

Florence sucks her teeth.

It's got to be said. I have to talk about the weather. It's expected. I want Cherise to experience the height of English conversation. She don't take tea so she'll have to bear a little of the British Labrish. (*Laughs nervously.*) Prepare her for what's ahead.

Florence But you going to fling it down on her one time. You come like a shower of rain! Tek time man.

Eunice Oh hush! Pour another in there.

Florence I thought you only stopping for one!

Eunice Well, I'm on a roll now, aren't I? Just pour will yer!

The two women laugh.

Don't mind us, Cherise. It's the same old carry-on ever since I've known her. Oh, I nearly forgot. (*She takes up her camera.*) Smile!

Florence and Martha pose together.

Another one for my wall. I'll give you a copy when I get them developed.

Florence You and your pictures!

Eunice Memories.

Florence (*sings*) 'Precious memories, how they linger . . . '

Eunice (*joins in*) 'How they linger in my soul.'

They laugh together.

Well, on me wall at home, anyway! And what's not on the wall ain't all that precious anyway.

Martha Thanks.

Eunice Well, that's enough of that! (*Gathering her bag and other bits and pieces that are around the flat.*) Well, that's me sorted! Is that blouse new?

Florence Buy it last week but it don't fit so good. The neck feel a little tight. Will have to move the button.

Eunice You're putting on weight, that's what. Mind she only has one piece of yam from that pot, Cherise!

Florence Stop yu noise! You have everything?

Eunice Well, if I've left anything behind I know it will be safe.

Florence Why don't you stay? Share the meal with us.

Eunice No.

Florence But . . .

Martha The woman have her business to do!

Eunice Will you stop! Honestly! I'll pop round next Wednesday as usual. Might bump into yer round and about. We'll be three next week!

Florence Yes. Of course. Another added to our number.

Eunice Got a brain like a sieve. She's forgotten that you are here already, Martha.

Martha I prefer Cherise.

Eunice Of course, Cherise! Sorry.

Florence So me mus use dis Cherise name too?

Martha Well, since you know me from time . . .

Florence Ah! . . . oh!

Eunice Oh! . . .

Florence Alright, Eunice! Thanks again. It was a big help. (*Gives her another kiss.*)

Eunice Not at all. Not at all. By the way, you've some messages on that machine of yours . . . OK Martha? Sorry . . . Cherise. See you soon.

Eunice and Florence go out to the front door.

Martha Alright.

Florence returns after bidding Eunice goodbye, closing the door behind her.

Florence You meet Eunice!

Martha Yes.

Florence A good friend.

Martha Can chat doh.

Florence So she stay!

Martha Is what we have dere? Irish potato?

Florence Calaloo and saltfish, dumpling and yam.

Martha Is what you saying? Me never know seh white people can cook dem someting! A dat kind a ting she cook all de while?

Florence Den is what you eat from yu come?

Martha Me try de chips and fish, get Kentucky. Eat a' couple restaurant when me was out shopping. Had a lovely Italian meal at a place near Oxford Circus.

Florence Can't remember the last time me eat at restaurant!

Martha Tink seh a Irish potato and raw meat me woulda get. Hear how English people can't cook. Like fe see blood a run outta dem meat. (*Makes a 'yukky' noise at this.*)

Florence A just de high top people who eat dem food so!

Martha No love my food cook well and must taste good. She seh me could come and have dinner wid she and her husband and her daughter. Me never know what me woulda get!

Florence When you wid a black man fe thirty-eight years what you expect? Him not gwine satisfy wid fish and chips every day.

Martha A true dat! Sound like she satisfy him wid more than her pot! Big ooman like that!

Places the food in front of Martha. They eat silently for a moment or two.

Fish could soak out little more . . .

Florence Taste good, man. Eunice cook nice. You eat yu food too fresh!

Martha Just like me mother.

Florence God rest her soul.

Martha Let's hope so. I don't really hungry. (*Pause.*) What dat flashing?

Florence Answerphone. Mek me hear who phone now.

Voice on Answerphone *Hi Mummy, it's me just to see if you got back yet. Life is fine this end, will phone at the weekend.*

Florence Angela.

Bleep.

Voice on Answerphone *Mum, I hope you had a good time. Let me know how everything went. I'm going to Barcelona this evening, got a last-minute flight so I'll try to ring from the airport. Alright . . . oh, say hi to Aunty Eunice. Tell her I saw Frankie last week. He's alright.*

Martha Must be David dat! You have to tell the kids them that I am here.

Two bleeps.

Florence True.

Martha They sound well.

Florence They are good children. Mek me proud.

Martha (*looking in the mirror*) De woman never ask me if me did want picture fe tek. I would tidy little and mek meself look presentable. Look pan me . . . favour a heng pan nail. Never even have time to put on little more lipstick and fix me head! (*Begins to preen in the mirror.*)

Florence You look alright. Just to capture the moment, soh she like to do it.

Martha Soh it go? Tings different.

Florence A noh England yu deh!

Martha Yes. Come and see how you stay.

Florence You see.

Martha Mm!

Florence (*with some unease*) Yes. Yes. Yes. Here since them move we out of Ingrave Street.

Martha Why yu did leave?

Florence Compulsory dem call it. Decide seh them going to mash dem down. All the work me work. Few pounds and a new flat.

Martha And deh England so long!

Florence So it go!

Martha Put me in the mind of the places that they build up in new Kingston! High up. So you can see all over the place.

Florence Me nu soh like de high living. Prefer a house.

Martha Is how it did stay?

Florence Nothing fancy, had a yard at the back and a front room. Never used to see much like up here but it was ours!

Martha Must be something like what me did see the other day when I tekking a walk I see some little houses board up over so! . . . Notice workmen was dere. Couldn't see if is fixing dem or dem getting ready fe mash dem down.

Florence Which side?

Martha Near the bar.

Florence And the school?

Martha Eh!

Florence I see . . .

Martha (*goes to the balcony window*) Watch train sah!

Florence Clapham Junction. Place can busy you see! The amount a train that pass through dat place. Going one place fe pass through again. Dem have one sign on a platform. 'Britain's busiest train station.'

Martha Famous! All me hear 'bout the place.

Florence Round here everything begin and end at the Junction. When we first come to Brixton in the sixties. All yu hear is Junction. Change your bus at the Junction. Go to the office at the Junction. Tek the train at the Junction. Never know seh is here me woulda end up at the Junction.

Martha Can go in all kind of direction. (*Looks around the room.*)

Florence Nah go no whey now. Dis is de final destination. The children seh me must move from here . . . but . . . don't know why . . . just feel to stay.

Martha Get used to a place.

Florence Yes, my dear. So how yu be?

Martha I all right. Glad to see you.

Florence Can't hear from yu. Don't know if yu living are yu dead.

Martha Like me was saying de business . . . tek up me time. It's hard work.

Florence Look like it pay off

Martha Yes. Come a long way from the one-room salon at Crossroads.

Florence Yu did name Martha den.

Martha I am still Martha, but well yu have add a gloss pan tings, yu know how it go. Fix up and smile . . . Fe de three long days of the competition! Will be good fe business when me go back. I thinking of trying my luck in New York.

Florence New York? Fe yu chest high, eh? Yu nu satisfy wid what yu have?

Martha 'Award-Winning Hairdresser' will look good on de advertisement. Dis is more than a trophy. American like dat kind a ting. People from back home need a nice place fe do dem hair and nail and ting! Plus you win prize and have something fe show. Can add a few more dollars to yu price dem and people happy to pay it. De trophy will look good in de new shop. A real selling point.

Florence Coming from afar.

Martha All de way from JA . . .

Florence Watch de gal who never like her hair fe comb!

Martha No . . . me never stay so!

Florence Yes . . . Mama used to comb your hair because yu wouldn't do it good . . .

Martha Fe true?

Florence Used to hear the bawling and the crying . . . never like your hair comb.

Martha Your memory good, eh? Me is a big woman now, don't feget dat!

Florence Never forget a thing.

Martha From so long.

Florence Not one thing. You want to sit on the sofa and relax?

Martha sits on the sofa. There is obviously a spring that is protruding, so she opts for the easy chair that Eunice was sitting in.

What time yu have there?

Florence Coming to five.

Martha Clock running slow. What you think of my present? I see the other one was just there and it not working . . .

Florence Is you bring it? . . . Some tings yu don't bother with. But I don't know if I would have chiming ting. Plenty noise. I don't have to pay too much attention to the time. It a pass by same way.

Martha (*looking around the room*) You have some nice little things. Plenty pictures of the children.

Florence Me blossom dem!

Martha (*picks up a picture*) David!

Florence Graduation last year.

Martha Blossom fe true! Look very handsome.

Florence Masters. I have two first-class degrees and a Masters! The children have done well!

Martha You never send this one, sis! Me don't have this one.

Florence I didn't bodder.

Martha What him doing again?

Florence No so sure of the proper title, some kind of computering business!

Martha Look at him! Face just a shine!

Florence Yes!

Martha I believe that photograph talk, you know?

Florence What yu saying?

Martha Yes. Like I see this one fe de first time now. See David stand up in all in him college glory. (*Adopts the same pose and uses a fake accent in a deep voice.*) 'I have the whole world at my feet, Aunty.' (*Laughs gently.*)

Florence (*laughs with her*) Yu nuh, right.

Martha Plus a journalist and an engineer!

Florence So yu did get the letter then!

Martha Oh yes I tek in all the news . . .

Florence One-way news doh!

Martha I don't have the time to write. (*Beat.*) You must be very proud.

Florence And de parcel dem.

Martha Every year.

Florence How are are your two?

Martha They not bad . . . Beverley working wid me now! A she me leave in charge. Euton still working fe the government. Doing OK. (*Silence.*) Not a bad little place at all.

Florence Small and comfortable. Easy to keep warm.

There is a silence.

Martha Imagine you fighting to keep warm and we fighting to keep cool.

Florence Imagine.

Martha My first visit to England.

Florence Fe six long months!

Martha (*defensively*) I don't have to stay so long.

Florence You always wanted to come to London.

Martha I glad that . . .

The phone rings

Florence Hello? You going to live long! . . . I was just thinking about you. You alright? Good . . . You reach before him . . . That's right . . . It was lovely! She really enjoyed it . . . Yes . . . Yes . . . What you going to do now? . . . Did you? What was she saying today . . . The same thing . . . That show! Anyway it pass the time . . . Of course . . . You go and look for Milly? . . . Seh what? When dem tek her in? . . . Which ward? . . . Me have to go tomorrow . . . Yes, of course . . . Me mind was running on her . . . Good job yu tell me . . . Alright . . . Yes . . . Later, Eunice . . . Bye and thanks. Thanks again.

(*To Martha.*) Eunice. Look at that. So it go all the while. Sometimes I am thinking about a thing, Eunice talk out exactly what I am thinking. Like we read each other mind. It is a funny thing. Take the other day. I look on this skirt a few weeks back but it was a little expensive so I leave it. Then Eunice come with by with my birthday box. The same skirt! Seh she get in the sale! I had was to marvel at the thing . . .

Martha You must did say something.

Florence (*emphatically*) No!

Martha So it goes sometimes . . .

Florence You want I put on the television?

Martha Alright.

Florence Something must be on that you will find interesting. While I wash up. Make yourself at home. Home from home!

Martha I will try.

Florence (*starts to clear the table*) Eunice and me move good man. We meet up every Wednesday and spend the whole day together. Sometimes just sit and chat foolishness. Sometimes is a little trip out or so . . . just something to pass the time. Mark you, we have plenty time . . . but then you simple surprise what can happen in the short space of time. Nothing and everything . . . the time can drag or it can go fast . . . You don't think so? . . . Martha? Martha?

We hear a children's programme going on in the background. Florence sees that Martha has fallen asleep. Florence takes a crocheted coverlet and covers Martha with it. She gently touches her head, and Martha shies away in her sleep. We hear a train rumble by and the faint sound of a train announcement.

Scene Three

In the flat. A few days later. Florence and Martha have returned from shopping in Brixton. They have an assortment of bags with them, including a few bedding plants. Florence is annoyed.

Martha After me never know!

Florence A England yu deh!

Martha Me know dat.

Florence Dis a nu Kingston!

Martha Bwoy me know dat too!

Florence When de people set up dem stall a fe people fe look pan! Dat is all!

Martha No ma dem a cheat and robber. Is how yu can have the best out fe show people and den sell them de rubbish? Is how that go? An when yu ready fe tackle dem 'bout it dem seh yu mus move from dem stall? Dem nu serious 'bout business inna England. Me sure of dat.

Florence A so tings go on here. I can never go back to that place! After all these years! Is there me go all the while!

Martha Shoulda a change long time! Mark you me nuh shop a market again! Me do all me shopping inna supermarket!

Florence A call de people all kind of bad word!

Martha Man upset me. I simple seh to him we want the nice oranges from the front! A tell me seh me can't have dem! How dat go? And me supposed to be the customer!

Florence Well, tings carry off different here!

Martha Different bredda! Different bad! And people sit down pan it? Dem could never do dat in Kingston or anywhere in Jamaica fe dat matter! Have de best outside and sell the rubbish and people nu raise hell 'bout it? No sah!

Florence Well, dis is how it go all the while. If yu mek noise dem may listen fe a while and then tings will go back to how it was. A soh me see it go from me come. And not a ting you can do about it!

Martha If everybody was mekking noise from long time, dem woulda haf fe change dem ways! But no. Stand up and accept it like pickney! And walk whey wid bad singing!

Florence Mek the best of what we have.

Martha Well, me would rather have nothing than mek compromise with me tings. Is how yu put up wid all dis?

Florence Never really consider it! (*Beat.*) Yu know something, yu stay one place and yu just watch things pass you by. You is here and yet you don't feel that you fasten on good. Just staying a while. Soon leave.

Martha Was coming back for my twenty-first birthday!

Florence See you now! Have two set a twenty-first and a look fe the third!

Martha Nu do me soh! (*Laughs gently.*) A 1948 me born, you know!

Florence So de tings dat used to bother me me don't pay them no mind for me soon gawn. Not stopping long. But me still deh ya!

Martha You could go now.

Florence To what?

Martha I'm dere.

Florence True. True. But me nu know yu again!

Martha Is how yu mean?

Florence De fancy clothes and de high living . . . me don't understand dat. Dis is where me reach. Dis is what me know. Likkle excitement on a Wednesday wid me good good friend. Me can't lef me pickney dem and de grand kids fe go sit down on a verandah whey me nu know nobody.

Martha Yu keep saying dat! I am yu one sister. Yu would make friends. People remember yu from de old days. Missus Williams big girl who went to England. People still ask after yu!

Florence Yes, when dem don't know what else fe say. (*Mimicking.*) 'How yu big sister, Miss Martha?' And whey yu reply? For yu don't know! Yu don't know nutting 'bout me. So me must pick up and falla yu and lef my life here?

Martha Yu did it once before. Lef me and Mama and come here.

Florence I come to me husband and de start of someting better.

Martha Yu coulda do it again.

Florence And leave me kids?

Martha Dem could come and see yu. Dem a big people!

Florence And me friends dem? Especially Eunice. I can't leave Eunice.

Martha Is whey yu and she have? Because of one little white woman and yu woulda stop here? People a pee inna de lift, fighting fe keep warm. Small balcony fe a garden. Yu don't have to live like this . . .

Florence Maybe is what I want. Some of us don't need whole heap of tings to mek us happy. Me not lonely and I satisfy wid what me have. Me can't start again in a strange place.

Martha Dat strange place is yu homeland! Is what dis place do to yu?

Florence stares at Martha for a moment and begins to unpack the shopping

Scene Four

Later the same day. The three are working out to 'Mr Motivator'. It is the warm-up section of the video.

Florence Him a little fast you don't think so!

Eunice (*puffing a little*) Not like Rosemary, is he?

Martha Mek it look so easy!

The three persevere and follow his instructions

No bredder, me can't tek nu more a dis.

She flops down on the settee, but jumps up quickly because she has sat on the protruding spring. The other two continue for a while longer.

Eunice Too much for me. I'll put the kettle on.

Florence I've started so I'll finish!

Eunice Will you stop!

Martha Eh! Extra!

Eunice Putting us to shame! What do you think you doing, training for the Marathon? (*Switches the video off.*) I'll bring Rosemary next week. Let's get the bun and cheese out.

She gets them out of her bag and goes to the kitchen for a plate, a knife and the butter, to prepare the snack on the dining table.

Martha Mek it the week after, me need time to recuperate after all dat. (*Begins to retouch her nail-varnish.*)

Florence Something we can manage. Rosemary more gentle wid we. Dis Mr Motivator man just a ackkle we up. Him a do exercise inna sunshine and nice sea breeze, him must feel good.

Eunice Not like us by a train station on a rainy Wednesday afternoon. (*Beat.*) Bun and cheese if yu please. (*Hands the snack around.*)

Florence Lovely. Dis will mek we feel better

Martha And dat's it fe afternoon?

Eunice There's a good film on later. One of my favourites, *Imitation of Life*.

Florence Yes man, when she bawl after her mother and a tell her she sorry!

Eunice But it's too late.

Florence Mm! (*Shakes her head, puts her hand to her heart.*) Oh yes! The bit that gets me is when she disowns her mother and she takes it in her stride and goes along with it and pretends to be her daughter's nanny.

The two women have a tear or two. Florence gets each of them a tissue and they dab their eyes.

Florence You going to enjoy dis film, Martha.

Martha I not so sure, look like it affect de two bad. (*Beat.*) What else yu do pan yu Wednesday?

Eunice Sometimes we go out.

Florence Don't have energy fe much else!

Eunice Speak for yourself, you! Not all my energy's gone. I've always a little in reserve for something or another!

Florence Keep quiet!

Martha I see.

Eunice Weather sometimes so awful that you don't feel like doing anything else. (*Beat.*) Sorted out the balcony? I didn't know you were going to do that this week? When did you go for yer bedding plants? I thought we were going next week?

Florence Martha's here, so I thought I would get on with it now. Get a few new bits and some of the plants needed re-potting. Some of them was pot-bound. Poor roots them have nowhere to go. But I don't know what to do with this one.

Eunice Put it by the door in the hallway That's where I've got mine – seems to do alright there.

Martha Not too dark and draughty? Dat's what you did tink, don't it sis?

Eunice No! It'll be fine. (*Beat. To Martha.*) Must make you feel homesick, seeing *Mr Motivator in the Caribbean*.

Martha Kinda.

Eunice All that space . . . fresh air.

Martha Can run to the beach any time you want. Sometimes after business finish. We go and cool down. Lovely.

Eunice Sounds like a good life. Must be lovely being able to live like that.

Martha Yes! I was talking to sis about dat only dis morning!

Eunice Really?

Martha She could come back wid me if she wanted to.

Eunice For a holiday? That would be nice. Few weeks in the sunshine.

Florence That is not what she had in mind.

Eunice Oh!

Florence Trying to inveigle me to go fe longer. Well for ever.

Eunice Oh! Bit further than Manchester isn't it?

Martha Get some sun in the old bones before she dead! She should go to her homeland. Lots a people doing it now.

Eunice Oh stop that!

Martha What would you do on a Wednesday if she go?

Eunice (*to Florence*) Will you go?

Florence I don't see it somehow. Something to think about doh!

Martha Yu pension would carry yu far. So me hear. Me have one an two returners who come to the shop. Dem look so nice and relaxed. Should come fe a holiday and see how tings stay. A little adventure.

Florence A mek plan fe me? But not having to have a winter coat and boots would be nice. Feel de sunshine. Dat would be lovely.

Martha Don't tell me dat it don't sound good?

Eunice Adventures can get you into a lot of trouble they can!

Martha Ever been? You and husband?

Eunice I haven't. He's been once or twice, taken our eldest with him . . . on one of his trips. They had a nice time . . . Doubt I'll get to go now!

Martha You should go and see what it is like . . . You could visit Florence when she come to stay.

Eunice You're right. But she's not going, are yer?

Florence Who is to tell?

Eunice It's money, though, see, and the invite . . .

Martha But you don't need invite when you dealing with family, just turn up and that's it!

Eunice Couldn't do that! Eddie says it wouldn't be a good idea!

Martha What yu husband 'fraid of?

Eunice What do you mean?

Martha Him tek a child and don't tek de mother?

Eunice Well, its not cheap you know. Was nice for Frankie to meet his grandparents, not like we're hopping over to Spain is it? Mind you, that would be a nice trip.

Martha You marry fe so long and you never meet any of your husband generation? Don't sound right to me!

Florence Martha, leave it alone!

Martha You husband love yu?

Florence Martha!

Eunice Of course he does! We've thirty-eight years together and six children to show for it! We've stuck together through thick and thin. What is all this about?

Florence Come Eunice! You know we Jamaicans! Just talk it out straight!

Eunice Well, it's not straight enough for me. What are you getting at?

Martha Me just wonder what kind a man have him wife fe so long and him people don't know her? Especially when him marry a foreign! Tings couldn't so bad dat you couldn't run fe one two week and seh howdy!

Martha He's not ashamed of me if that's what you think!

Florence Nobody saying that.

Eunice That's what I'm hearing! (*To Florence.*) Well, what do you think, I don't hear you saying anything. (*Beat.*) For once!

Florence I never give it much thought.

Eunice So why do you think I haven't been invited?

Florence Dat's between you and yu husband.

Eunice I'm asking you!

Florence Yu done seh de money ting is a worries.

Eunice There's something else! I know there is.

35

Florence Is what? You tell me.

Eunice You people can close ranks when you ready! Clam up and can't get a bleeding word out of you.

Florence Who yu calling 'you people'?

Eunice Her! You! Him!

Florence Stop dat!

Eunice Always the bleeding same, I just want to get in there, be part of the conversation, and I'm locked out, like you say, 'Don't come any further . . . ' It's been like that ever since we've met. Kept at arm's length . . .

Florence It's been for your own protection.

Eunice Protection? Protection from what?

Florence Me seh too much areddy!

Eunice Finish what you were going to say. Protection from what?

Florence Well, when you did come round here first time . . .

Eunice Just before we got married . . . and?

Florence People had the wrong idea about you . . .

Eunice Yes?

Florence Your kids out playing till all hours . . .

Eunice What about it?

Florence They used to call you all kind a name. I stand up for yu doh . . . the one white woman in the street. I mek sure yu never hear what dem used to seh . . .

Eunice Which was . . . ?

Florence Well, yu like fe talk 'bout de bed department and such . . . dem used to call yu a prostitute.

Eunice Is that right? I was larking about, having a laugh. Yu know that.

Florence They didn't . . . Dem never like it and believe seh a only prostitute talk like dat . . .

Eunice That right?

Martha Birds of a feather flock together, you never know that?

Eunice And it's always the cuckoo that comes along and upsets things in the nest!

Florence Martha, stop that!

Eunice All yer talk about holidays. We were quite happy before yer came and we'll be a lot happier when you've gone!

Florence Eunice! You have no right to talk to her like that . . .

Eunice Nobody asked you to come here.

Martha I am family, I don't need invitation.

Eunice Are you sure you're welcome?

Martha I am family!

Eunice Yes, and when I told her that Cherise had come to see her she didn't bloody well know who you were!

Florence Enough now!

Eunice My Eddie loves me. He does! I know he does. I don't know why I haven't been with him to Jamaica. (*To Florence.*) We haven't had a cross word in years and now this!

Martha Just talking.

Florence Never see yu like dis before.

Eunice Well . . . I never needed to be like this before . . . until now. I don't like it when you shut me out . . .

Martha A discussion. That's all. Getting to know we one another better.

Eunice (*supping her tea*) Mm! Well, maybe I know all I want to know. And what I don't know, I don't need to! I'm off!

Florence So soon! Is only three o'clock, the film soon start.

Eunice I'll watch it at ours. (*She leaves.*)

Florence Eunice!

We hear the door slam shut.

Why yu couldn't keep quiet?

Martha I ask a question, dat's all!

Florence Yu really upset her. (*Beat.*) And me. I know that woman fe a long time.

Martha She show her colours today doh!

Florence She did get mad dat's all, what could she do? I must go over there, smooth things over.

Martha Smooth what? Leave her! Yu sure yu need a friend like that?

Scene Five

Later that same day. Eunice has returned to the flat. Martha is not there. She has come to collect her bag and her video.

Eunice So where is Miss Cherise then?

Florence Some of her hairdresser friend come fe her and them gone somewhere. All a dem poshed up. She put on frock she seh she buy from Harrod's.

Eunice (*impressed*) Oh!

Florence Have on sandals with rhinestone all over them. So is somewhere fancy.

Silence for a moment.

Sorry about earlier.

Eunice She touched a nerve. And you did.

Florence Yes.

Eunice Well, more than one.

Florence Yes?

Eunice This talk about taking you with her.

Florence It's talk.

Eunice I'd hate that. How can one person come and unsettle everything? She looks so bright and breezy, plenty of money, and not a care in the world. It seems full of sunshine, reminds me that I live in the shadows. I'm sure she doesn't like me.

Florence Stop that! She don't know you.

Eunice Seems like she is striving and it's paying off. Makes me jealous, I'll tell you.

Florence Don't be.

Eunice Then about me and my Eddie. I'm making polite conversation and she goes WHAM! Right to the heart of it. Just what I've been thinking for years. Is this man proud of me?

Florence Yu God wid yu! Stop that!

Eunice I have to ask the question.

Florence Yu and him still deh! What yu talking about?

Eunice I have to wonder. We had our 'adventure' when I was sixteen. If I'm honest I would have never married him. I was curious, I'd heard all sorts about darkies. I thought, 'one time', and then I would know. I wasn't a virgin. I hadn't been caught, so I thought well . . . why not? It would be a laugh. Something to tell the girls at break time. None of the others dared to do what I was going to do. I was going to have that man and dump him after a while. When I got fed up of him I'd say 'Ta-ra,' then that would be that, on to the next one. Our Frankie was on the way before that could happen. I didn't know how to stop him. The 'blousey girl' from Chapeltown was having a darkie's baby.

Florence Him never leave yu.

Eunice 'I will do de right ting.' So he did. Eventually. After three kids. A move down south out of the way. You know, when our Frankie was born he promised that he would take the two of us home to meet his mam. I were that pleased! Well, before I knew it our Cheryl and Valerie were on the way. A cheap ring from Woolies and a wedding reception for me twenty-first.

Florence So . . .

Eunice So . . . Cherise Sylvester comes in and hits it home. It's never going to happen.

Florence Not everything go according to plan. I know dat.

Eunice I had so much hope that it was going to be alright

Florence And now . . .

Eunice Now . . . I please him in the only way I know how. That keeps him happy. I cook him nice dinners and make sure he has a clean shirt for going out. (*Beat.*) If it wasn't for you I couldn't even do that! Taught me how to cook. How to look after a black man . . . didn't have a clue.

Florence I was just helping you out. Don't mind.

Eunice (*tearful*) I try not to, but I'm getting fed of trying. (*Beat.*) At least I can keep you company. Makes it easier somehow, knowing you are just across the way.

Florence Have more company than me know what fe do wid at the moment.

Eunice Now there's a truth.

Florence Me nu know dis Cherise and me nu so sure dat me want to either.

Eunice She is a bit . . . I don't know, a bit 'top drawer'.

Florence Stoosh! Dat's the only word! Too stoosh!

Eunice How long is she staying?

Florence God to tell!

Eunice Haven't yer asked?

Florence Me can't ask dem kind a question, mam. When she ready she will go. Problem is me ready fe her fe go now!

Eunice She's not been here that long. What, a couple of weeks?

Florence Dat long enough! Just have to mek the best of it!

Scene Six

It is two or three weeks later. Martha is on her own in the flat. The furniture has been changed around quite significantly in an attempt to make a little more space in the room.

We hear some of the latest sounds from Jamaica playing. Martha is doing her hair and is getting ready to go out.

Eunice has just arrived.

Eunice When did she say she will be back?

Martha I not sure. When she come I tell her say that you call.

Eunice I'll wait. How are you then?

Martha Fine. Recovered from our little trip.

Eunice Well, you've had fish and chips at Brighton! You've hit the high life! We'll go every year, me and Florence. Have done for years. Go for a little paddle and that.

Martha Nice place.

Eunice It's alright. (*Beat. Indicating the change of furniture positions.*) Someone has been busy!

Martha Yes, is me. Sis don't see it yet, I think this way will give her a little more room. Think she will like it.

Eunice She doesn't know?

Martha Surprise for her when she come. Did a little cleaning too. Mek her comfortable.

Eunice I see.

Martha What you doing here?

Eunice Just passing. Like I normally do.

Martha I see.

Eunice I don't think it makes that much of a difference. I'm not sure that she'll like it!

Martha Enough to give her a little more space to stretch out her legs when she is watching television and from here she she can see her flowers. Then there was all this old rubbish she have behind the settee. (*Indicating a few boxes.*) Well, not all of it old but . . . I didn't feel seh I should dash dem whey! She can sort it out when she come.

Eunice I see. Thought it through, then. (*Looks in the boxes.*) There's one or two things here she will want to keep I'm sure. (*Picking up a pair of gloves.*)

Martha Just seeing things with a fresh eye. That's what was needed.

Eunice I'm sure these are the gloves she wore at my wedding! She was my witness and I remember she got really dressed up in a sky-blue suit with navy shoes and handbag to match.

Martha Yes? I believe she did send that picture home.

Eunice Made me feel quite shabby and I was supposed to be the bride! (*Laughs. Beat.*) That was a lovely day. (*Beat.*) Going anywhere nice?

Martha Going to see a cousin in Vauxhall later this evening.

Eunice Yu cousin Gladys? Yes, I know Gladys . . . Send howdy will yer?

Martha If I remember.

Eunice Must be wonderful to be able to do your own hair. Make it look nice and then to be able to do hair for others and get paid for it . . . the best of it.

Martha You could be right.

Eunice Have you done Florence's hair?

Martha No. Not yet.

Eunice That's an idea for a Wednesday session! Get our hair done.

Martha People pay me a lot of money to do their hair.

Eunice Well, you could experiment . . . You're a world-class hairdresser, try out some of the English styles for when you go back. (*Laughs.*)

Martha (*laughs*) I don't see no style from I come . . . none that I would want to tek back anyway . . .

Eunice How was your time with Angela?

Martha Very nice. She seems to be doing well. Living in a big apartment . . . overlooking water. Very nice.

Eunice Lovely girl, isn't she? Done her mother proud. Mind you, I never thought being an engineer was quite the right thing for a girl to be doing . . .

Martha Something different. Tek me and her mother all round London. Get to see Buckingham Palace.

Eunice Very good. Nice to see these places before you go.

Martha These places that you hear about and yu see pon de TV. Very strange.

Eunice Oh?

Martha Looking at Buckingham Palace, Houses of Parliament or Trafalgar Square, places that so familiar yet unfamiliar. You know them but you don't know them. Whenever I seen dem places is in a book or pan de TV when someting special going on. Funny, now that I see them the places not as I imagined or them fancier than I thought.

Eunice Are you disappointed?

Martha Yes and no. Excuse me. (*Leaves to go to one of the bedrooms to get dressed. From the bedroom.*) But I want to know something.

Eunice What's that now?

Martha How the Queen wid all her money can't get curtain fe fit the windows at the Palace properly?

Eunice Can't say I noticed. Not been into London for a long time . . .

Martha The net curtain all bungle up, and just rest on the window sill. Them don't look good at all.

Eunice I expect there is a very simple explanation.

Martha Then we did go to Piccadilly Circus . . . the hub of the Empire, dem used to tell we in school . . . one little statue . . . and plenty dirt and muck round de place . . .

Eunice Still, you're glad you've seen it . . . ?

Martha (*returning dressed and looking spectacular*) An experience.

Eunice Eh, that's a looking lovely dress . . . You look a million dollars . . .

Martha Dat's the idea. (*Turns so that Eunice can zip her up.*)

Eunice Good job I was here!

Martha Yes.

Eunice But then I always am . . .

Martha Dat's a truth! (*Beat.*) About the other week . . .

Eunice Don't you worry yerself . . . all blown over now.

Martha Ah, so me stay. Just bawl out what me tinking . . . never mean anyting by it.

Eunice Like I say, don't worry. It's a sore point at ours.

Martha An yu don't do anything about it?

Eunice Yu can't teach an old dog new tricks.

Martha Old or not, him woulda have fe learn. Not easy me know, but me learn . . . and see me yah!

Eunice Go away with yer! Yer not that old.

Martha Nineteen forty-eight me born. Work it out.

Eunice Really? Which month?

Martha August.

Eunice We're practically twins! My birthday is in May. You've kept well. (*Examines herself in the mirror.*) You'll have have to tell me your secret.

Martha Good living and hard work, that's all.

Eunice Well, I've had the hard work! Still waiting for the good living. (*Laughs.*)

Martha You and my sister!

Eunice You work with the hand that fate has dealt you.

Martha Sometimes you need to ask question. And ask them good. You born and grow here. Not like Florence.

Eunice Still a stranger all the same. In a place and that's where you stay. Unless you've been lucky like some of my kids. To move out and on. (*Gives a great sigh.*)

Martha Oh yes?

Eunice Of my six kids there's only one nearby. One in Canada, another says she's travelling but been in Australia for months. The others left London. And our Gemma, well she won't leave home . . . never leave home.

Martha An yu can't move out or on?

Eunice Too late. Too late. Like one of them old trains that they've stopped running. Parked up in a siding. See them all the time from ours. (*Lets out a nervous laugh.*) Yu fancy a drink?

Martha No, but yu mek yourself comfortable!

Eunice Home from home for me here. (*Goes to the kitchen.*) I'm not passing through.

Martha What word yu throwing?

Eunice I don't know what yer talking about.

Martha Yes! Talking 'bout passing through.

Eunice I just think, well, you're here then you will be gone.

Martha And you will still de bout?

Eunice Well, I have been for nearly forty years. Like family we are.

Martha Yu push up yuself dat's what. Don't give her likkle ease.

Eunice Like I say. Family.

Martha You could never be family!

Eunice A Christmas card once a year? That's what makes a family? Tell me something. What's her favourite flowers?

Martha How me woulda know something like that?

Eunice Roses. What's her favourite colour?

Martha Red.

Eunice Yellow.

Martha So dem deggae information put you in a better spot dan me?

Eunice No. I just been here!

Martha And I've been there! Just a different spot.

Eunice What are you talking about? Better? Different? It's not a competition!

Martha Ah, yu a turn it into one. All me hear morning noon and night from my sister is Eunice. How she know yu an yu know her, and how she don't know me! Like a my fault! A nu she come a England and never come home, but fe one time? Den start mek complain that no one know her? A she mek herself strange. We was dere a wait fe she.

Eunice I'm sure you were. (*Beat.*) How much longer have you got here?

Martha Yu a run me? (*Beat.*) Couple more weeks I think. Not so sure. Month pass a reddy and not much going on.

Eunice Done lots a shopping!

Martha True enough. Spend lots of money on meself and sis won't tek anyting from me.

Eunice Mm . . . she's very proud is our Florence. If you ask, she says no, but if you bring it in then she's glad to see it. It's always the same. Do you know when we go the seaside on our days out, like the other week, it's always the same, she will spend her last penny on yer and never tek anything in return. But if I just turn up with an ice-cream or a bag of candy floss or summat like that she's that pleased! She never stops thanking me all the way home. That's the way she is!

Martha I see. I want to get something nice for her before I go. What you think she would want?

Eunice Well, I know she could do with a new coat for the winter.

Martha Dat's all?

Eunice Maybe you could put a pair of boots with it. That would be nice.

Martha Cho' I want to give her a real present, man, something that she look on and seh, well, when my sister was here she give me this!

Eunice Well, we did see some lamps the other week when we were out. She called them the Dallas lights . . . they'd go well in here . . . mind you I don't know where you'd put them . . .

Martha Dallas lamps! And a new settee! All the move me a move tings around it nu look any better inna de place. Me see some nice one at the place whey she get did dis one.

Eunice Arding and Hobbs . . . you'd buy her a sofa?

Martha Yes man! Is a good idea.

Eunice I don't think so!

Martha Of course it is.

Eunice Believe me!

Martha Get rid of all dis old junk and replace tings new. Mek she really comfortable and feel good.

Eunice Florence likes to keep things just so. Have a word with her before you do anything.

Martha Yu done seh that she not gwine tek it like dat if me talk to her 'bout it.

Eunice There's a world of difference between a bit of candy floss and a sofa. Look, I know her better than you do . . .

Martha You telling me how to treat my one sister?

Eunice I didn't mean . . .

Martha We is off the same vine and fig-leaf. I know she will like my idea. Improve tings for her!

Eunice I just wanted . . .

Martha Don't talk to me about who you know well from who you don't know. Me and my sister is one blood. Just because you live 'genst her and me live far don't mean seh that there isn't a tie between us!

Eunice Bleeding hell! If I can just get a word in edgeways! Let me just put the record straight here!

Martha She deserve better dan dis!

Eunice Look, I didn't want to upset yer! I was just saying when you are with people day in and day out you kind of have a different view. That's what I meant . . .

Martha You just jealous. 'Fraid seh my sister place going to nicer than yours when I finish wid it.

Eunice Alright! Alright, I'm going to keep out of it!

We hear the door bell ring excitedly. It is Florence in the hallway.

Florence Hello! Hello! Sorry I tek so long. (*Noticing the changes in the room.*) But stop! Is my flat dis? Don't look bad at all!

Martha Yu like it?

Florence (*sitting on her sofa, carefully putting a cushion on the protruding spring*) Get a good view of me flowers from here so! Eh! Eh! Foot can stretch out! What is dis! Is fe who idea?

Martha I me fix it up so!

Florence Nice, nice. What yu tink Eunice?

Eunice I did wonder if . . .

Florence It lovely, man. Really nice. Hey hey, come clear from Jamaica wid new ideas, eh? Look pan dis Eunice and never tink fe change tings.

Eunice No. Never did.

Florence Well, if a just fe dis me glad yu come! My likkle sister come and a sort me out. So how are things?

Eunice *and* **Martha** Fine!

Florence What a way you hair look nice. And dress up like you going nightclub! Just visiting we visiting. A begging yu do mine fe me What you think, Eunice?

The clock chimes five.

Yu see dis clock? A chime every minute.

Eunice (*laughs*) Every hour! It chimes every hour.

Martha (*laughs*) Yu can exaggerate, eh? Ah so she stay from time!

Florence Minute or hour. When yu leaving tek dis ting wid yu, me nu know if me can tek dis noise a me ears all de while!

Martha Me can't tek back a present, I will get stye in me eye!

Eunice Wouldn't want that!

Florence No! Not at all. The Number One hair-stylist wid chigga pan her face!

Martha Wouldn't be good fe business.

Florence Imagine!

Eunice Yu couldn't set up a new fashion!

Florence People a come to yu shop and seh, 'I'll one of those please!' Go a New York and set up a new trend!

The three are laughing at their nonsense.

Florence So when yu will do fe me and Eunice hair?

Martha Soon! Before me leave.

Florence Eunice, we going to step out sharp. We have to find somewhere to go and show off! (*Laughs.*)

Eunice You'll be sharper than you think!

Martha You have yu chat and yu bun and cheese. I feel fe a likkle fresh air . . . look around the shops and fatten me eye dem.

Eunice Just mind you don't spend all yer money!

Florence Don't stay too long! (*To Eunice.*) Leave her alone. She is on holiday.

Martha 'Bout time I have a little adventure of my own . . .

Florence Sound like me when I first come . . . couldn't wait to step out on my own . . . mark you won't find any gold on the streets . . . me been looking for a very long time . . . (*Laughs heartily.*)

Eunice A very, very long time . . .

Florence Alright.

Martha Me gawn!

Eunice How's Milly?

Florence (*returning to her conversation*) Going down fast, don't look she going to make it to the end of the week . . .

Scene Seven

Later that week. Martha is in the flat on her own. She is on the telephone to Eunice.

Martha . . . She's gone to see someone in hospital . . . Ah who? . . . Dat's right . . . Milly . . . Next week . . .

Wednesday nuh yu usual time? I want the two of you to go out . . . Nu bodder wid Mr Motivator! . . . of course it going to work. I will just 'sick' so I can't go. They seh I must let them know whether morning or afternoon . . . What yu tink? . . . Alright so come back early evening . . . You have to, man . . . Tek a extra cup of tea somewhere other . . . Yes . . . Don't start that . . . She will like it, I know dat . . . Alright, we have the plan see . . . Don't let me down, Miss Eunice . . . oh!

Scene Eight

The following week. Florence has returned, as arranged, from a shopping trip with Eunice and enters her flat to see a new three-piece suite. It is a showy affair, in yellow leather. She looks at it incredulously. She walks around the sofa, almost not daring to touch it. She is about to sit on it, but decides against, and sits on a dining chair instead. She puts on a Jim Reeves LP. We hear Martha return. She has brought Kentucky Fried Chicken.

Martha Evening!

Florence Evening!

Martha What you tink? (*Beat.*) When me gawn yu can sit down in comfort and remember me.

Florence When all dis plan?

Martha Likkle while ago. Yu like it?

Florence What yu do wid me rest of tings?

Martha People dem gawn wid it. What yu tink? Yu favourite colour!

Florence So me see. Is why yu do dis? (*Begins to cry.*)

Martha Don't bodder wid that, man! We coming from afar. You like it? Yellow.

Florence So me see.

Martha And the lamps. Dallas style.

Florence Alright.

Martha Yu nah seh much.

Florence Mm . . . dem look nice . . .

Martha Dese are a little smaller than de other one dem. You have more space now.

Florence Could be.

Martha Will tek some getting used to.

Florence Fe true.

Martha Where you want to put the sofa? Shall I leave it here? It could go over so . . .

Florence I don't know

Martha Little after this we move tings to your suit. People seh there is a ten-year guarantee. Good amount of time.

Florence If me last so long.

Martha I must look out for something like this when I go back. Ting pretty man. Nice and comfortable. (*Sits in one of the chairs.*) But stop. What yu doing sitting on the dining chair? Sit down an try out de ting, man!

Florence I don't tink so. Nothing was wrong with the other one.

Martha Stop yu noise! You like this kind of settee. Remember we did admire something like dis when we was out de other day.

Florence The other one was alright!

Martha No spring fe stick up in a yu crotches! Nice smooth leather.

Florence (*strokes the sofa*) No warmth!

Martha So wha' wrong?

Florence I don't want it!

Martha What yu saying?

Florence I want back the old one.

Martha You mad? De people gawn wid it. Fancy furniture. Darling, dem don't come fancier dan dis! Me can tell you dat! You have good taste.

Florence You shoulda save yu money

Martha Don't worry 'bout dat, man!

Florence I will decide what I worry about! You tek it upon yourself fe tek whey me few tings whey me work hard for and replace dem all unbeknownst to me and me must 'nu worry'?

Martha I don't understand. The old settee you have from when! A turn museum piece inna de place . . . you wanted this one.

Florence Just a dream . . .

Martha A dream come true!

Florence Dat settee was de start and the finish! (*Begins to cry.*)

Martha You have something new . . . Start again.

Florence Me too old fe dat . . . me did expect fe fade whey wid me few tings round me. Can't come too soon!

Martha Stop dat!

Florence Come a show off . . .

Martha No!

Florence Wid yu shopping trips and you fancy clothes. A big up yu self!

Martha A nu soh it go . . .

Florence Yes! What I have nu good enough! Whey me live small! You tink I don't hear yu? England too quiet. Place dutty.

Martha I can speak as I have a mind!

Florence Well, dat is what me doing!

Martha 'Bout time. I don't know what wrong wid yu!

Florence Imagine! Buckingham Palace want fix up! Not even whey de Queen live good enough!

Martha Just talk me inna talk!

Florence Can't fix up Buckingham Palace so yu start pan my little place! Tek whey me tings. Don't ask no question!

Martha Help mek tings better fe yu.

Florence Tings woulda been better fe me coulda look straight. All the while. I have to looking back. Mama have enough? Martha school fees pay dis term? When letter come from JA me heart sink . . . Is what dem want now?

Martha A noh why yu did come?

Florence 'Dear Sister Florence . . . I begging yu dis and, sis, I begging yu dat!'

Martha I needed the help dem time.

Florence So when I put me foot down and tell yu seh yu must satisfy wid de one parcel a Christmas and anyting dat me can send, yu stop write! Twenty years I only get Christmas card from yu. Because you can't milk de ole cow no more! Malice me off because I say enough is enough!

Martha I just needed a little more help to get me out of a hole.

Florence I been doing that fe de last forty years.

Martha You in deh a England. Me tink seh tings was better here!

Florence The help I was giving you to get out of a hole meant I was pushing myself into a deeper one!

Martha You never help when I really needed it!

Florence (*shouting*) Because me know seh I was throwing good money after bad! Yu was always needing help. It would never stop. You would never amount to anything! I was tired!

Martha Ah! So dat's the belly bottom of it? Well, look! See! I mek it. Without you! Mek me own way! And better dan yu. Dat's what hotting yu! Don't it?

Florence Whatever yu is or whatever yu have, me have a hand in it!

Martha Stop yu noise! Whey yu was when me haf fe a work and look after Mama? Whey yu was when me haf fe get up soon and tek care of my kids them and then stand up fe twelve and fourteen hour fe a few dollar a day?

Florence Me send money fe help and me send me parcel dem. Every year, never miss!

Martha Yu an yu blasted parcel dem! Pure cheap foolishness! Fe de longest while I don't mek use of anything yu send! Most a de tings dem me give to people who really need dem! The better something me sell dem fe get whey me want!

Florence Seh what? I deprive meself fe mek sure I send tings.

Martha Trouble was yu sending de wrong tings. A nu toothpaste and ugly dress material me did want dem deh time! Mama mighta satisfy wid dat. Me did want whey me inna ask for. Nu whey yu have a mind fe send me! So don't tell me yu have a hand inna my success! No help. Me one and me pickney dem! No husband! No mother! And no help from you just when me did really need it. Me haf fe do all kind of sinting fe mek sure me have money fe products fe do people hair!

Florence Like what?

Martha No mind! I did what I did haf fe do! Yu see how life sweet fe me doh! Can wear any frock me want. Nu haf fe consider. Can sport and run 'bout de place. What you can do? Just want to heng on to old time tings, when people spend dem money bring quality inna yu life. Hot me! Just accept de ting. Is something dat yu need, not even want. Need!

Florence You know what a hotting me? Dat I can still see yu! I want see yu arse come outta a me place! Nobody did invite yu here!

Martha No! Soh me have fe invite meself! I woulda dead if me inna wait pan yu.

Florence An maybe yu shoulda dead a long time ago. Me woulda been living in a mansion wid de amount yu get outta a me instead of dis likkle piece of place. Come out! I gwine tank God nuff when yu gawn back a Jamaica!

Martha You nah tank God more than me, darling! If dis a treatment me a get? Me will sort out me ticket and den me gawn. You really turn wrangside.

Florence What ever yu doing, do it quick!

Martha Since a so yu start it won't be quick enough!

Florence Eh! Me nu start yet! (*Grabs one of the new lamps.*) See again what would a mek me happy! (*Opens the balcony door, throws the lamp out and grabs the trophy.*)

Martha A wrong wid yu?

Stops her from throwing the trophy. Florence slaps Martha's face.

Florence Get out a me sight! Yu bitch! Come out a me place! Get out! Nobody did ask yu here. Nobody!

Martha leaves hurriedly and in an upset state.

Scene Nine

It is later the same day. Early evening. Florence is still sitting on a dining chair, and staring into space. There is a box of photographs and papers next to her. She has been looking through them since Martha left. Eunice uses her key to get in. The radio is on.

Eunice Light not working?

Florence Better like dis.

Eunice I'll put the kettle on, shall I?

Florence Need more than tea at this moment.

Eunice Maybe. But it's a start. I've got a very hurt sister over at ours.

Florence Can't hurt more than me. Look what she do me dear mam? Tek whey me tings.

Eunice She's replaced them.

Florence Wid show tings.

Eunice Something you 'wanted'.

Florence Talk. Me never get what me want.

Eunice That's exactly what I said. Bought these. (*Hands her photographs.*) Keep meaning to bring them over.

Florence You did know 'bout de plan?

Eunice She did mention something.

Florence And yu never stop her.

Eunice Me? Stop Cherise? I know my limits, love! 'Want to mek my sister happy.' Who am I to put a stop to that?

Florence De settee!

Eunice Aren't you just a bit glad about this one?

Florence I worked hard for thar settee.

Eunice So . . . Now you've got another one.

Florence Gwine hard fe kip clean. Show up every likkle mark!

Eunice Why don't you just accept it? The other one was getting a bit past it.

Florence Yu deh pan her side

Eunice I'm on nobody's side. It is a lovely settee!

Florence You know how I have to suck salt out of a wooden spoon to get that settee. Leave the kids them sleeping early morning gawn fe clean. Run back to see to them. But it was worth it. Have a nice front room. Every little thing in there. Pictures and de gram. Somewhere fe sit and consider de progress that me an Archie mek. Sit and joke. Place clean and shine. Happy days. Till we did have to move.

Eunice No choice.

Florence See it dere. I don't have place to put tings as I have a mind. Tings still in boxes since I come here over twenty years ago. Like me. Coop up inna box. Shame it not smaller. Done wid it all.

Eunice Stop that talk. She was trying to help. Wanted to make you happy.

Florence Me is the one that do the happy making, dat's what me did come here for!

Eunice Tables turned.

Florence An' I don't like it. Not at all. Is how she manage it? A million JA in the bank!

Eunice I know. Shouldn't be worrying about things like that. That's where dreamin' gets yer, I suppose.

Florence Work hard and still vital, same way like when we was young.

Eunice You haven't seen her for what . . .

Florence Too long.

Eunice It's a lot to catch up on . . .

Florence Like I don't know her.

Eunice You've written, sent pictures . . .

Florence A one-way street. And there's plenty of things between that I don't even bother with . . .

Eunice Not with you . . .

Florence Like I just give her the headlines like Fay write in her newspaper . . . 'David get him Masters'. 'Fay moved to Manchester.' 'Archie dead.' 'I move.' I never bother with the small print . . . you know . . . the little things that mek the story . . . the tings that carry life along . . . like the trouble I had was to find a suitable hat for the Masters ceremony or how I cry all day when Fay left. Remember? Or how I couldn't cry over Archie. And I still not giving her de details, like how me see me house standing for ten years and dem just pull it down today an how me upset 'bout it.

Eunice Well, maybe now is the time to share that.

Florence Dem seh that absence makes the heart grow fonder. (*Grunts.*)

Eunice True. True.

Florence An a next one. How it go? (*Thinks a moment.*) 'Bout contempt.

Eunice Familiarity breeds contempt?

Florence Ah! you have the right one deh so. Familiarity breed contempt. A noh so it go. Dem have dem the wrong way round. Should be 'Absence breeds contempt.'

Eunice 'Familiarity makes the heart grow fonder' has a certain ring to it.

Florence Me have a stranger living wid me for the last few weeks. Somebody me hardly know. De fancy frock and the big hairdos ting whey we couldn't have. Space between us is bigger than the ocean she just fly cross. We just a mek small talk like yu do wid people when yu just a see dem fe a likkle while.

Eunice It all takes time.

Florence And it roll over so quick.

Eunice You should be enjoying it. Think on. You might not see her again. Not unless they double the pension or I win the lottery. It's hard, I know.

Florence You could be right. (*Sighs.*) I just . . . wonder how things would have been if I had stayed home?

Eunice Probably nothing much.

Florence Wouldn't know you.

Eunice That would have been devastating! (*Gives her a big hug and holds her close.*)

Florence If yu was a man I could really love you.

Eunice I know, I know. I love you too. Very much.

Florence If tings had been different.

Eunice Another place. Another age maybe.

They look at each other and kiss and hold each other for a while.

What am I to tell her?

Florence Not really sure . . . I don't know.

Eunice If you don't know, then neither do I!

Scene Ten

It is much later that evening. Florence is ready for bed. She is still sitting on the dining chair, drinking a cup of hot chocolate. Enter Martha. She has taken her make-up off and is in her night clothes. Martha goes to the kitchen and get herself a drink. It is obvious from their demeanour that they have been in the flat together for some time.

Martha Is what yu do since me leave here?

Florence Leave yu leave or run me run yu? (*Beat.*) A sit and consider! So yu spend the whole of the time at Eunice?

Martha Yes. Get dinner and everyting. She and Eddie really look after me.

Florence Yu lucky . . .

Martha What yu was considering?

Florence How me reach here? Soon seventy. Tings should be different. Me a look pan dese. (*Picks up a selection of photographs.*) There was so much promise.

Martha We did see it.

Florence Forty-odd years and me a still wait fe de promise.

Martha (*reading from a letter*) 'I hope these few lines reach you in the best of health . . . ' (*Smiles to herself.*) You keep these after all these years?

Florence Feget seh dem was there. Have dem behind de settee. Don't know why I hanging on to dem. (*Beat.*) Wonder yu never mek de people tek dese too!

Martha Little remembrances. Like Eunice and her pictures.

Florence Her pictures are living memories. But dese . . .

Martha (*interrupting*) Look, the three of us! I have mine on my dresser.

Florence All dressed up and going nowhere.

Martha One last picture together. Next day you gone!

Florence Mm . . .

Martha Off yu went . . .

Florence . . . and end up here.

Martha Could be worse.

Florence Eh! And could be a lot better an' all.

Martha Yu was seeing little life . . . me and Mama used to love to get yu letters dem.

Florence Well, sometime letter and picture can't tell the whole story. When yu look at this picture what it seh to yu?

Martha Seh?

Florence (*adopting the pose in the photograph*) I gawn! When I come back I can buy the whole of Kitson Town if I want!

Martha (*adopting her pose*) Just me and Mama now!

The two women look at each other. Martha continues to rummage through the box.

We did have people a England. Tings was good fe we!

Florence A soh it go. I did what I could.

Martha Which was everyting as far as Mama was concerned. (*mimicking her mother*) 'I know I can put on my pot fe boil and run to the post office. Letter from England will be dere. Can buy few tings and come home and eat till me belly full!' (*Beat.*)

Florence (*looking over Martha's shoulder, sees another picture*) Eunice wedding! See the gloves?

Martha Me hear talk bout dis!

Florence (*putting on the gloves, adopts another pose*) Me foot burning me! I don't know what I doing here. (*Pause.*)

Martha (*concentrating on the photograph*) What a way she look, prosperous!

Florence I don't finish pay fe dese shoes yet! See what happen when you go further than yu can reach?

Martha I miss my sister.

Florence I miss my sister. Eunice seem nice . . . I need a friend right now . . . Dat's a fact.

Martha holds a tearful Florence for a moment or two.

Martha Better than me. Little life did see me at that point. (*Laughs gently at her joke.*) Little life see me. Was there with Mama. Had was to stay.

Florence Yes.

Martha I decide that when I get a chance I was going to do something fe meself. Be like my big sister. Dress nice. Live in a nice place. Somewhere famous.

Florence Clapham Junction!

Martha Well! I was going to make it. I sure of that. Couldn't understand. You couldn't come home to see Mama fe the very last time.

Florence Yu come and see. At the junction. Always seem to tek the wrong turning. Seemed to get further away from me destination. De children come along. Another junction, mek another plan. Archie lose him job. Another junction. Another idea. Dem tek whey we house and put we here. Another junction. Nu bodder again. Getting home wasn't going to happen again. Just rest me self and satisfy.

Martha I used to wonder. How people deh a England so long and a send back tings . . . and can't come . . . ?

Florence Yu getting an idea. (*Beat.*) Couldn't give out the whole story. The children used to read a story about Dick Whittington and him cat and how him come to London to seek him fortune.

Martha Yu did send something like that for my two.

Florence Don't rightly remember how the story go but de kids used to say, 'Dat's what yu did, Mum, you and Dad came to London to seek your fortune!'

Martha Bright kids.

Florence I used to smile and couldn't tell them that like Mr Whittington Cat, me bury de filth and was sitting on it so that dem couldn't find it. Remember how puss dig a hole before dem go a toilet and cover it when dem done? Dat's what I been doing. Smelling it an hiding it. From de kids. From you. From Mama.

Martha Mama wouldn't have understood . . . (*Begins to mimic Florence.*) 'Yes Mama . . . I come . . . I come . . . couldn't mek yu go without me send yu off . . . I know . . . I know. See me here . . . See me here . . . '

Florence Oh God!

Martha I am . . . the bigger one . . . I will tek care of her . . . Where she is? She just outside . . . Martha! Martha! Mama want tea! Put on that pot . . . Put on that pot!

Florence Stop it! Stop it!

Martha Mek sure that water nice and hot. Mama want a nice hot cup of tea . . . Call me. Call me when it boil . . . I going to mek the cocoa tea just how yu like it . . .

Florence Martha! Stop, stop!

Martha Tek time now, tek time . . . you rest, yu rest! I'm here, I'm here . . .

Florence is sobbing.

Once she hear yu voice she just slip away . . . Had a smile on her face. Peace at last.

Florence And torment fe another.

Martha At least now it share. (*Lets out a sigh.*) I wanted yu to hold on to. I needed yu to bawl wid! I felt so poor. I still do. Me did feel mad wid yu. Yu should have been dere.

Martha is hugging herself. Florence takes her in her arms.

Had to send her on her way.

Florence Yu do the right thing.

Martha I did do a double grieving dat day. Mama gawn and you weren't there.

Florence I couldn't be.

Martha Me know dat. (*Beat.*) Now. Just wanted to mek tings better fe yu. My turn. We've lost so much.

Florence Time. And dat running out again.

Martha It's more than time. Look how yu and Eunice move. Know nuff 'bout yu one another. Whey yu like from whey yu nu like. Can go buy frock fe yu. I couldn't do that.

Florence Don't know meself. Just a move from day to day. Like me deh pan the wheel we ride on the other week.

Martha Just looking straight.

Florence Yes ma . . . just looking straight, wasn't sure what I was looking for but I just hold me head straight . . . (*Beat.*) when me could hold on and hope that one day tings will turn.

Martha But it was all bad?

Florence No! The road was more crooked than straight doh. Never really know what the prize was supposed to be. Come to England! The motherland needs you! Was expecting something. Something. Just when yu feel seh yu reach, the rules change up and yu have to enter another competition. The prize seem so far way. Tek such a long time to gather tings and mek progress as we sort out dem seh we have to move. Fe development. Is only today dem start break dem down. I stand and I watch how dem tek down in a few minutes whey we did tek years fe build. Only bricks and mortar. But still. At least me did have me few tings. Tings whey me work for. Likkle reminder that tings was going right. Fe a while. Nearly reach the end of the rainbow. Nearly ketch one of de prize. Favour yu ketch it and never have fe leave go nowhere.

Martha Staying in the same spot mean seh me a own somebody. Whey me born and grow. Sometimes I used to tink when tings start turn fe me, 'Sis did run whey too quick.'

Florence Or de call did come too early. What could I do? Had to come. Archie wanted me and Fay wid him.

Martha Natural.

Florence Mama needed help. You in school. It was the best ting. At the time.

Martha Shoulda come home.

Florence Wid three English pickney? No sah!

Martha At least it woulda a easier.

Florence I don't tink so.

Martha Kids woulda a get used to tings.

Florence Couldn't tek dat chance. Dem was doing well in school. (*Beat.*) De one ting dat work out.

Martha True enough.

Florence So I just work and hope seh tings would different fe dem . . . or de grandkids . . . or maybe the great-gran . . .

Martha You a look far, eh!

Florence Just holding the hope. (*Beat.*) But look what one fancy settee can do? Deep deep chatting fe de longest while.

Martha Come nuh! (*Tapping the sofa.*)

Florence (*sinks into the sofa*) The leather just sigh! (*Beat. Leans over and gives her sister a kiss on the cheek.*)

Martha When me gawn yu can remember me every time yu sit down.

Florence When yu gawn. I begging yu someting.

Martha What again?

Florence Don't seh goodbye.

Martha Seh what?

Florence I don't want hear goodbye from yu. My friend Milly who me work wid her fe de longest while. Nu have long now. Somehow the goodbye me a give her start fe get hard. Don't know when I will bid her de last.

Martha Mm! Harder still when yu know seh it is de last.

Florence My dear!

Martha 'Just go on de balcony.'

Florence What?

Martha De last word yu did seh to Mama! She repeat those words over and over on the way from the airport.

Florence Poor substitute, eh? And dat did pain me. Couldn't kiss her or anything. I had an idea dat it would be the last time.

Martha Never plan fe come back?

Florence Archie did just lose him job. Me never know what was going to happen. Save a little heartache. (*Beat.*) Was bad enough when me did leave de first time. Tink seh me heart was going break. Never want to leave but had to.

Martha Me was just excited, we have people going to England. Yu shoulda hear how me a show off to me school friends dem.

Florence A de farewell singing! (*Sings.*)

> When for a while we part,
> This thought will soothe our pain,
> That we shall still be joined in heart,
> And hope to meet again.

Me heart breaking as me a sing.

Martha 'Blest be the Tie.' I sing dat so often sending people off. Sometime I used to tink dat the tie was a curse and a blessing.

Martha But yu couldn't break it.

Florence No.

Martha And now?

Florence Well, the tie is a blessing and a curse and I don't want to break it.

Martha No.

The two women hold each other close. The phone rings.

Florence Hello? Alright . . . No, she nu dead . . . Not yet! (*Laughs.*) Tanks! Alright? Later!

Florence *and* **Martha** Eunice!

They both laugh gently.

Scene Eleven

We see Florence enter the flat. She has a new hair-do which she admires in the mirror. She switches on the television.

Florence She must soon come.

She switches on the television, and begins to set the table for two people. As she is doing this the six o'clock news starts, and she realises that the clock has not chimed: it has gone. She goes out to the bedroom and comes back. Martha has gone. She sees the trophy in the corner with a note stuck to it.

(*Reading the note.*) This is yours.

Florence surveys the trophy. Lights fade.